GCSE Edexcel
Core Science
Foundation — the Basics
The Workbook

This book is for anyone doing **GCSE Edexcel Core Science** at foundation level, with a predicted grade of D or below.
(If you're not sure what your predicted grade is, your teacher will be able to tell you.)

It's full of **useful practice questions** to help you **get to grips with** the essential science you'll need for the exams.

And of course, there are some daft bits to make the whole thing vaguely entertaining for you.

What CGP is all about

Our sole aim here at CGP is to produce the highest quality books — carefully written, immaculately presented and dangerously close to being funny.

Then we work our socks off to get them out to you — at the cheapest possible prices.

Contents

Published by CGP

Editors:
Luke Antieul, Katie Braid, Charlotte Burrows, Emma Elder, Mary Falkner, Felicity Inkpen, Helen Ronan, Jane Sawers, Hayley Thompson, Jane Towle, Karen Wells, Sarah Williams, Dawn Wright.

Contributors:
Paddy Gannon

ISBN: 978 1 84762 714 8

With thanks to Edmund Robinson and Glenn Rogers for the proofreading.

With thanks to Jeremy Cooper, Ian Francis and Ann Shires for the reviewing.

With thanks to Jan Greenway, Laura Jakubowski and Laura Stoney for the copyright research

www.cgpbooks.co.uk

Printed by Elanders Ltd, Newcastle upon Tyne.
Clipart from Corel®
Based on the classic CGP style created by Richard Parsons.

Classification

Q1 a) Draw lines to match each **kingdom** to a **feature** of the organisms in that kingdom. One has been done for you.

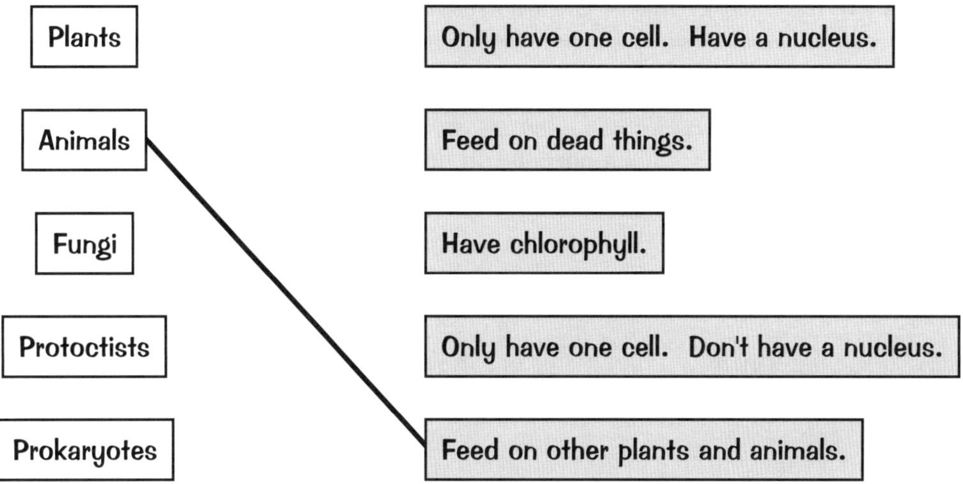

b) Which of these kingdoms is made up of organisms that **don't** have **cell walls**? Circle **one** answer.

PLANTS ANIMALS FUNGI

c) Why don't viruses fit into any of the kingdoms?

....

Q2 The chart below shows how scientists split kingdoms up into **smaller groups**.

Fill in the gaps using the words in the list below.

genus order class species

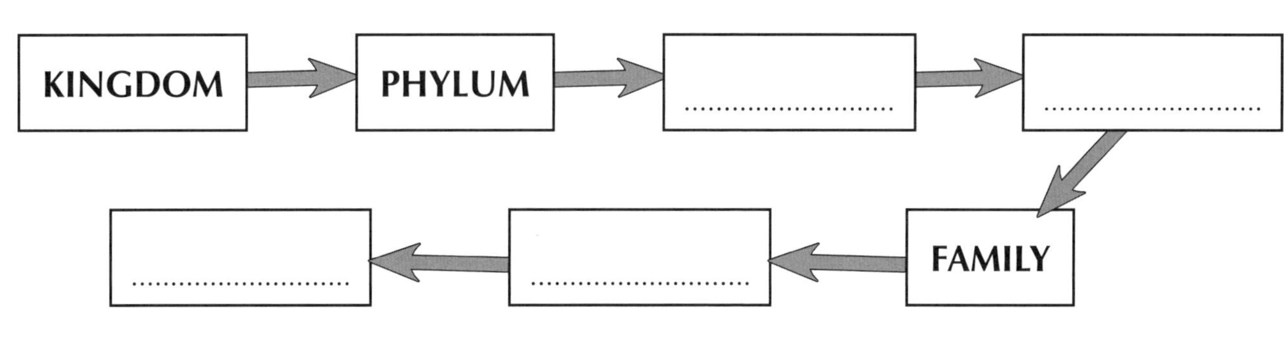

Classification

Q3 a) Circle the word to complete this sentence.

A phylum is a group of organisms with **no** / **some** characteristics the same.

b) What do all the animals in the **phylum Chordata** have? Circle **one** answer.

feathers | a supporting rod up the back of their body | six legs | really good hearing

Q4 How do you know if two organisms are the **same species**? Tick the answer.

They can have children and the children are not fertile. ☐

They look the same. ☐

They can have children and the children are fertile. ☐

Being fertile means that you can have children.

Q5 Carl finds this **leaf** on a path.

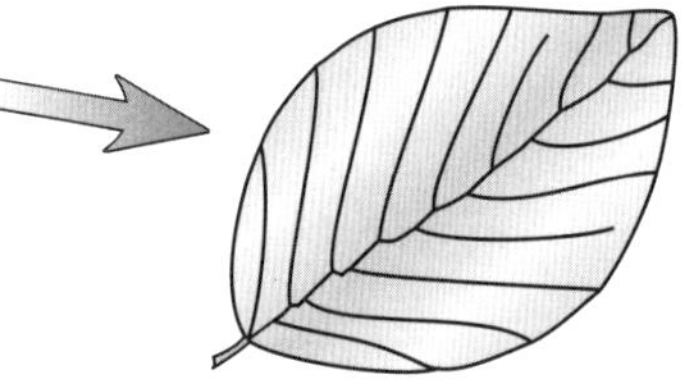

Use the **key** below to work out what type of tree the leaf is from.

KEY:

1. Is the leaf long and thin?	Yes – it is a WILLOW tree leaf No – go to 2.
2. Is the edge of the leaf smooth?	Yes – it is a BEECH tree leaf. No – go to 3.
3. Is the leaf wider at the top than at the bottom?	Yes – it is a CHESTNUT tree leaf. No – it is a BIRCH tree leaf.

Type of tree: ....

Vertebrates

Q1 a) What are **vertebrates**?

....

b) Circle the **three** main things that scientists use to put vertebrates into groups.

how they take in oxygen | how they take in minerals | how they reproduce | how they control their body temperature | how they control their blood sugar level

Q2 Draw lines to match up these words with their meanings.

VIVIPAROUS | Laying eggs

OVIPAROUS | Giving birth to live young

Q3 What ways might a vertebrate **take in oxygen**? Circle **three** answers.

through their stomach | through their skin

through gills | through their eyes | through lungs

Q4 Tick the boxes to show if these statements are **true** or **false**.

		True	False
a)	Animals that are **homeotherms** have warm blood.	☐	☐
b)	Animals that are **poikilotherms** have warm blood.	☐	☐
c)	Mammals have cold blood.	☐	☐
d)	Reptiles have warm blood.	☐	☐

Genes and Chromosomes

Q1 Circle the right words in the sentences below.

a) Chromosomes are found in the **cell wall** / **nucleus** of a cell.

b) Your chromosomes carry your **genes** / **cells**.

c) Genes are **bigger** / **smaller** than chromosomes.

Q2 Write the correct label on each diagram.

a)

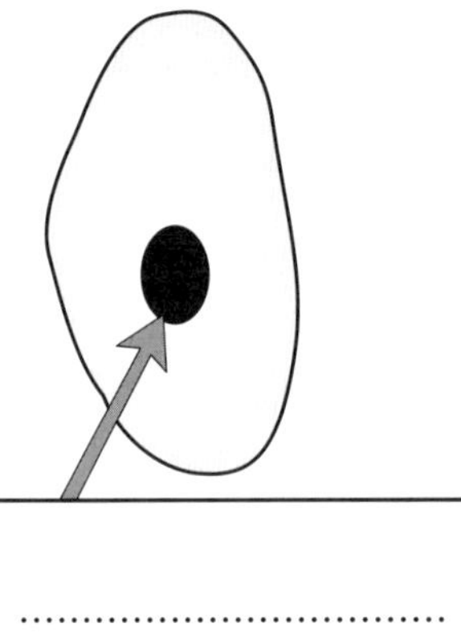

b)

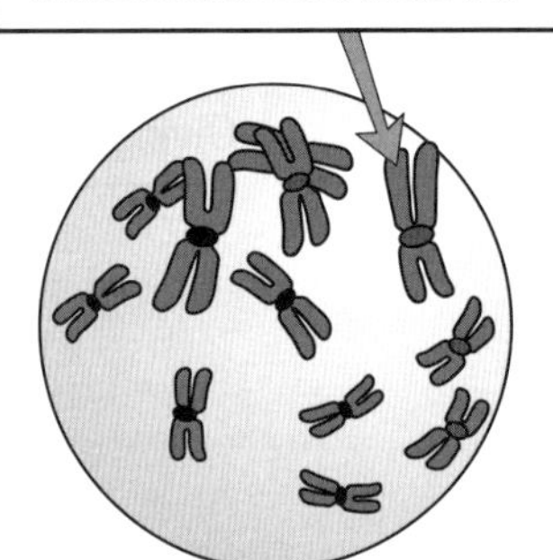

c)

Q3 Tick the sentences that are **true**.

- Genes carry chromosomes. ☐
- Genes control what characteristics a plant or animal has. ☐
- The same genes control different characteristics. ☐
- You get your genes from your parents. ☐

Variation

Q1 a) Tick the sentence which is **true**.

☐ Differences in characteristics are caused by the environment only.

☐ Differences in characteristics are caused by genes and the environment.

☐ Differences in characteristics are caused by genes only.

b) Complete the sentence using one of the words.

Differences in characteristics are called ....

cloning **variation** **reproduction**

Q2 Tick the boxes to show whether these statements are **true** or **false**.

		True	False
a)	Everyone has the same genes.	☐	☐
b)	You get a mixture of genes from your mum and your dad.	☐	☐
c)	The height of a plant is controlled by its genes and the environment.	☐	☐

Q3 What is a mutation? Tick the answer.

A mutation is a change in heart rate. ☐

A mutation is a change in the weather. ☐

A mutation is a change in a gene. ☐

Q4 Helen and Stephanie are identical twins. This means they have the **same genes**.

Helen weighs more than Stephanie. Is this because of her genes or her environment?
Circle the answer.

her genes **her environment**

Continuous and Discontinuous Variation

Q1 Draw lines to match up these two terms with their meanings.

Discontinuous variation is when

Continuous variation is when

a characteristic can have any value within a range.

a characteristic has a set number of different types.

Q2 Greg grows **pea plants**. The graphs below show the **length** of the pea pods and the **colour** of the peas.

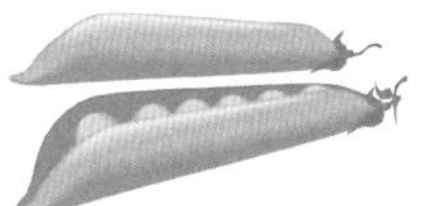

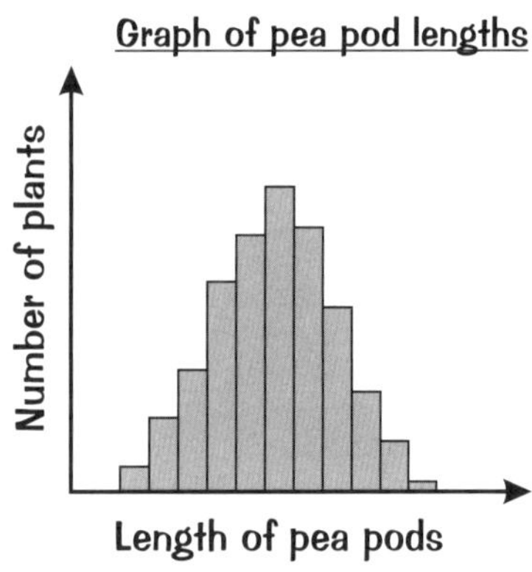

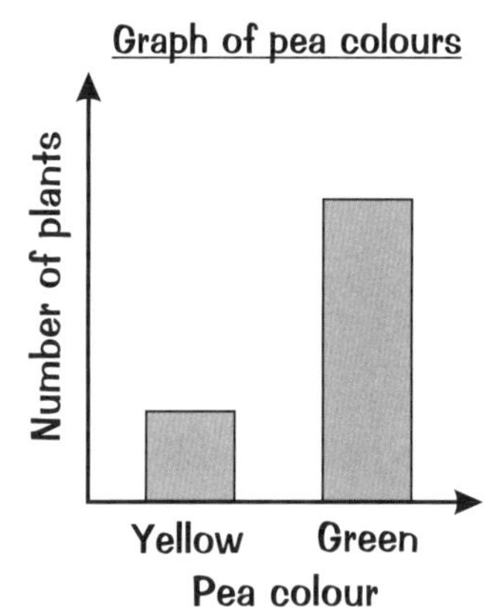

a) Which of the characteristics showed **discontinuous** variation? Circle the answer. length of pea pod / pea colour

b) Which of the characteristics showed **continuous** variation? Circle the answer. length of pea pod / pea colour

c) Most of the pea pods had a length that was about average. True or False? TRUE ☐ FALSE ☐

Q3 Eve asks everyone in her class what their **blood group** is. Her table of results is shown on the right.

Blood Group	Number of people
A	8
B	4
AB	1
O	10

a) What was the **most common** blood group? ☐

b) Is blood group an example of continuous variation or discontinuous variation?

....

Adaptations

Q1 The picture on the right shows a **polar bear**.
They live in the Arctic where it is **cold** and **snowy**.

How do these **adaptations** help the polar bear to survive in the Arctic?

a) Having a thick coat of fur.

....

b) Having white fur.

....

Q2 Some bacteria and animals live near **hydrothermal vents**.

a) What is a hydrothermal vent? Tick the answer.

- A dip in the rocks at the bottom of the sea where cold water gathers. ☐
- A crack in the rocks at the bottom of the sea that gives out hot water. ☐
- A small underwater mountain that is covered in coral and seaweed. ☐

b) Why is it difficult for things to live near hydrothermal vents? Circle **two** answers.

the water is very cold | the bottom of the sea is under high pressure | the bottom of the sea is under low pressure | the water is very hot

Q3 Penguins are adapted to living in the **Antarctic**.

a) Why do penguins have oily feathers?

....

b) This graph shows the average monthly temperature for a place where some penguins live.

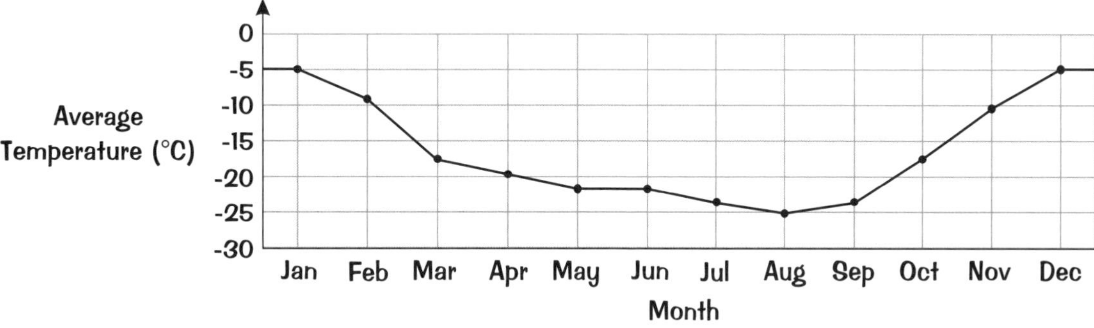

August is the coldest month. What is the average temperature in August? ....°C

c) Circle **one feature** that helps penguins to survive at this temperature.

sharp beak | lots of body fat | webbed feet | good hearing

Natural Selection and Evolution

Q1 Who came up with the idea of natural selection? Circle the answer.

Isaac Newton   Charles Darwin   Elizabeth Gaskell   Marie Curie   Lamarck

Q2 Complete the sentences to show how **natural selection** works.
Choose words from below the lines. The first one has been done for you.

There is ....lots of.......... variation between living things of the same kind.
lots of   no

a) Most living things have .... young. Not all of them survive.
lots of   a few

b) Living things .... with each other to get the things they need to survive.
compete   breed

c) Some of them have characteristics that make them more likely to survive.

This means they're more likely to .... and pass on their characteristics.
breed   die

d) Over time these characteristics will become more ....
common   useful

Q3 **Big ears** help a **rabbit** to **hear predators** coming more easily.

a) Look at the two rabbits on the right.
Which rabbit is more likely to **survive** and **breed**?

....

A   B

b) What is likely to happen in the future?
Circle the correct sentence.

In the future there will be more rabbits like Rabbit A.

In the future there will be more rabbits like Rabbit B.

In the future there will be no rabbits.

More about Evolution

Q1 There are **three** main ways that scientists **check each other's work**.

Draw lines to connect each term below to its correct meaning.

Conferences	Magazines where scientists can read about each other's work.
Scientific journals	A scientist gives their work to other scientists to check before it's put in a journal.
Peer review	Meetings where lots of scientists discuss their work.

Q2 Circle the right words to complete these sentences.

The **more** / **less** closely related two species are the more similar their DNA is.

Scientists can look at DNA to work out how species **went extinct** / **evolved**.

Q3 **Warfarin** is a **poison** that was used to **kill rats**.

a) Some rats are resistant to warfarin.
What does this mean? Tick the answer.

- They are killed by warfarin. ☐
- They are not killed by warfarin. ☐
- They cannot eat warfarin. ☐

b) "The warfarin resistant rats are less likely to survive and breed." True or False? TRUE ☐ FALSE ☐

c) Choose a word from below the line to fill in the gap in this sentence:

Over time the number of warfarin resistant rats has ....

increased decreased

Alleles

Q1 The nucleus of a cell has **chromosomes** in it. Chromosomes carry **genes**.

a) How many copies of each chromosome are in a cell? ☐

b) How many copies of each gene are in a cell? ☐

c) What are alleles? Tick the answer.

- Different versions of the same gene. ☐
- Genes that are identical. ☐
- Genes that are dominant. ☐

Q2 Draw lines to match the terms below with their meanings.

genotype	having two different alleles for a gene
homozygous	having two alleles the same for a gene
phenotype	the actual characteristics you have
heterozygous	what alleles you have

Q3 a) If both alleles are **dominant**, which characteristic will be shown? Circle the answer.

the recessive characteristic   the dominant characteristic

b) If both alleles are **recessive**, which characteristic will be shown? Circle the answer.

the recessive characteristic   the dominant characteristic

c) Which characteristic will be shown if one allele is **recessive** and one allele is **dominant**? Circle the answer.

the recessive characteristic   the dominant characteristic

Q4 Eve has the alleles **Bb**. This means that she has **brown eyes**.

a) Is Eve **homozygous** or **heterozygous** for this gene? ....

b) What is Eve's eye **genotype**? ....

c) What is Eve's eye **phenotype**? ....

Genetic Diagrams

Q1 In cats the allele for black fur (**B**) is **dominant**. The allele for brown fur (**b**) is **recessive**.

a) Two cats have kittens. Complete the diagram to show the alleles the kittens could get.

Father cat

Bb

B b

Mother cat Bb

	B	b
B	BB	
b		

b) What colour fur will kittens with the following alleles have?

BB .... Bb .... bb ....

Q2 The allele for **dimples** (**D**) is **dominant**. The allele for **no dimples** (**d**) is **recessive**.

a) Jody and Mike are having a baby.
Complete the diagram to show the genes the baby could inherit.

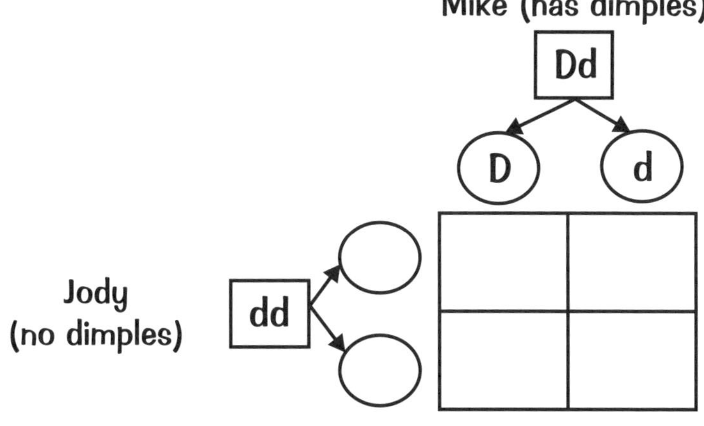

b) Will children with the following alleles have dimples? Write '**yes**' or '**no**'.

Dd .... dd ....

c) What is the chance of the baby having dimples? Circle the answer.

25% **50%** **75%** **100%**

Genetic Disorders

Q1 Write down two **symptoms** of **sickle-cell anaemia**.

1. ....

2. ....

Q2 Libby has **cystic fibrosis**.

a) Is cystic fibrosis caused by a **dominant** allele or a **recessive** allele?

....

b) Circle two **symptoms** of cystic fibrosis from the options below.

breathing problems   low blood pressure   ear infections   lung infections

c) Libby's sister is a **carrier** of cystic fibrosis. What is a carrier? Tick the answer.

Someone with two copies of the dominant allele.	☐
Someone with only one copy of the recessive allele.	☐
Someone with two copies of the recessive allele.	☐

Cystic Fibrosis

Q3 The **family tree** below shows a family with a history of **cystic fibrosis**.

Karl
Susan
Billy
Anne
Malcolm
?
Baby

Key:
Male
Female
Sufferers, ff
Carriers, Ff or fF
Normal, FF

a) Is Susan a **sufferer**, a **carrier** or is she **normal**?

....

b) What alleles does Malcolm have? ....

c) Could Billy and Anne's baby have cystic fibrosis? YES ☐ NO ☐

Mixed Questions — B1 Topic 1

Q1 The **arctic fox** is adapted to living in the arctic.

a) What features help it keep in heat? Circle **three** answers.

a thick coat | big eyes | a long tail | long claws | lots of body fat | a round shape

b) The fox has white fur. How does this help it survive? Tick the answer.

☐ It helps the fox to dry off fast when it gets wet.

☐ It makes the fox hard to see. This means it can sneak up on its food.

☐ It helps the fox to reflect heat, keeping it cool.

c) Circle the right words to complete these sentences about how the arctic fox evolved.

An arctic fox with white fur is **more** / **less** likely to survive and breed.

This means that it is likely to pass on **white** / **black** fur to its babies.

Over time arctic foxes with white fur became **more** / **less** common.

Q2 Martin has two **geese** called Gary and Dora.

a) Geese belong to the animal kingdom.
Tick **two** features of organisms in the animal kingdom.

☐ Have lots of cells (are multicellular).

☐ Have a cell wall.

☐ Only have one cell (are unicellular)

☐ Are heterotrophs (feed on plants and other animals).

☐ Have chlorophyll.

b) Geese are **oviparous** animals. What does this mean? Circle the answer below.

they lay eggs | they have live young | they have lungs | they have cold blood

c) Gary and Dora have babies.
Their babies are not fertile.
Are Gary and Dora the same species?
Tick the answer.

YES ☐ NO ☐

Mixed Questions — B1 Topic 1

Q3 **Cystic fibrosis** is caused by a **recessive** allele (**f**).

This diagram shows a cross between Max and Tina.

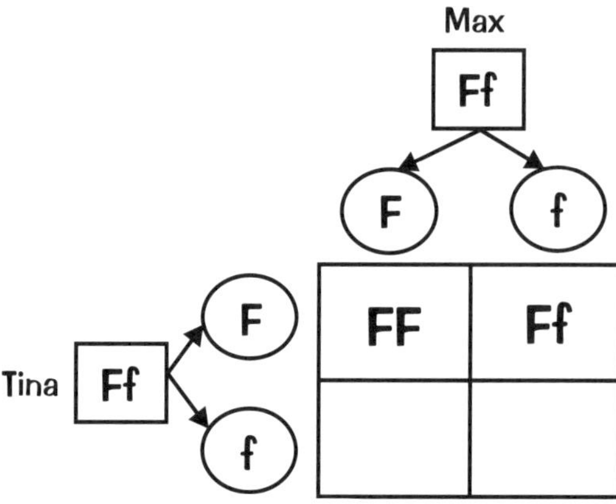

a) Fill in the two empty boxes on the diagram.

b) Max and Tina are having a baby. What is the **chance** that the baby will be a **sufferer**? Circle your answer.

0% 25% 50% 75% 100%

c) Tina has the alleles Ff. Circle the box that best describes Tina.

normal a carrier a sufferer

Q4 Pea plant flowers can only be **purple** or **white**.

a) Peas are in the **plant kingdom**.
Do their cells have cell walls? ....

b) The allele for **purple** flowers is **P**. The allele for **white** flowers is **p**.
Tick the boxes to show whether these statements are **true** or **false**.

	True	False
The allele for purple flowers (**P**) is **recessive**.	☐	☐
A plant with the alleles **Pp** will have **purple** flowers.	☐	☐
A plant with the alleles **PP** will have **purple** flowers.	☐	☐
A plant with the genotype **pp** is **homozygous** for the **white** flower allele.	☐	☐

c) Is pea flower colour an example of continuous or discontinuous variation? Circle your answer.

discontinuous variation continuous variation

Homeostasis

Q1 What does **homeostasis** mean? Circle the answer.

A — Keeping conditions outside your body the same.

B — Keeping conditions inside your body the same.

Q2 Draw lines to match up these words with their meanings.

OSMOREGULATION	Controlling body temperature.
THERMOREGULATION	Controlling how much water is in the body.

Q3 Tick the boxes below that are next to **true** statements.

The hypothalamus keeps your body temperature steady. ☐

When you're too hot, blood vessels in the skin get wider. ☐

When you're too cold, you sweat. ☐

Sweat is made by adrenal glands. ☐

When sweat evaporates it takes heat from your skin. ☐

Q4 Choose a word from below the line to fill in the gaps in these sentences.

a) When you are too .... your body hairs stand on end.
warm cold

b) Muscles called hair .... muscles make the hairs stand on end.
erector reactor

c) This traps .... to help keep you warm.
water air

Neurones

Q1 **Neurones** carry messages around the body.

a) Circle the word to complete this sentence:

Neurones carry information around the body as **chemical** / **electrical** impulses.

b) Where two neurones join together there's a **tiny gap**. What is this gap called?

....

c) What are the **chemicals** that carry information across the gaps called? Circle the answer.

receptors **neurotransmitters** **myelin**

Q2 a) Label the parts of the **neurone** below. Write A, B C and D in the boxes.

A synapses

B myelin sheath

C axon

D dendrons

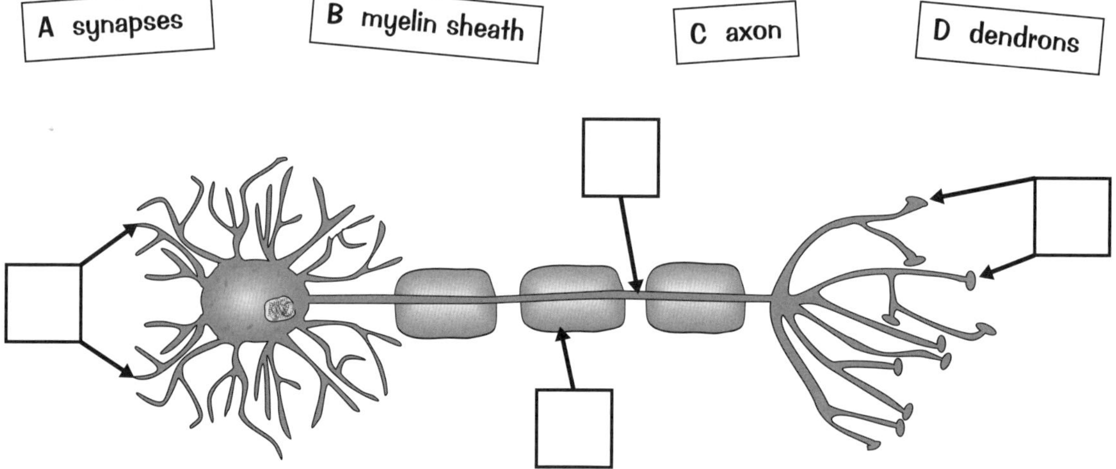

b) Draw lines to match these **parts of a neurone** to **what they do**.

Axon	This stops the impulse getting lost. It also speeds up the impulse.
Myelin sheath	The impulse travels along it.
Dendrons	These branches let the neurone connect with lots of other neurones.

The Nervous System

Q1 What is a **stimulus**? Tick the answer.

A change in your environment which you may need to react to. ☐

A cell that carries messages to and from the central nervous system. ☐

A type of sense organ. ☐

Q2 Tick the sentences that are **true**.

You have three sense organs. ☐

Sense organs have different receptors in them. ☐

Receptors are groups of cells that detect a stimulus. ☐

Q3 Fill in the table to show what each **sense organ** has **receptors** for. Use the words from the list.

Ears Taste Skin Eyes

Sense organ	Receptor type
	Light
Nose	Smell
	Sound
Tongue	
	Hot and cold, touch, pain

Q4 The **CNS** decides what to do about a stimulus.

a) What do the letters **CNS** stand for?

....

b) Circle the **two** main parts of the CNS.

brain eyes spinal cord liver receptors

The Nervous System

Q5 a) What do **effectors** do?

....

b) Circle **two** types of effectors shown below.

glands ears brain muscles

Q6 Draw lines to match up the name of the **neurone** with the description of what it does.

Sensory neurone	Carries an impulse from the CNS to an effector.
Relay neurone	Carries an impulse from a receptor to the CNS.
Motor neurone	Carries an impulse from a sensory neurone to a motor neurone.

Q7 The picture below shows an **impulse** going through the **nervous system**.

a) Fill in the labels on the diagram. Use words from the list below

CNS Effector Receptor

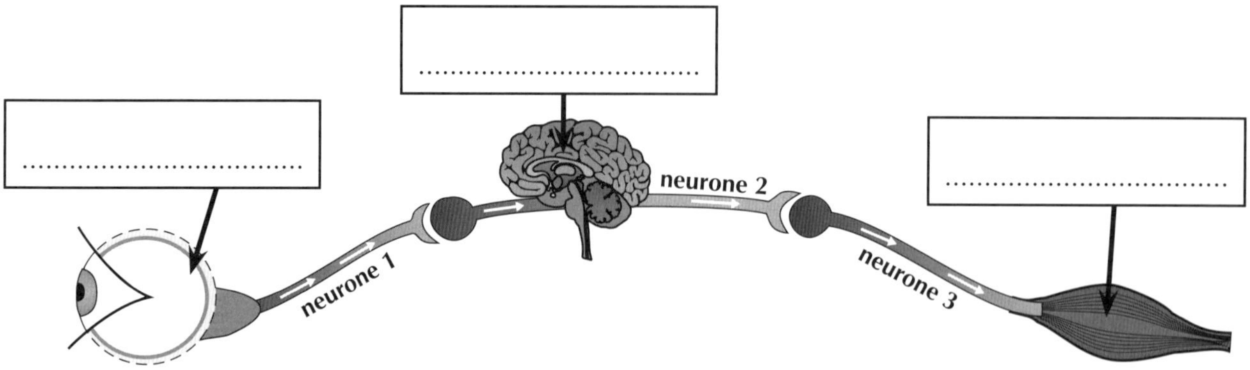

....

neurone 1 neurone 2 neurone 3

b) There are three neurones shown on the picture.
They are marked as neurones 1, 2 and 3.
Which of these neurones is a **motor neurone**?

Reflexes and Stimuli

Q1 Circle the correct words in the sentences below.

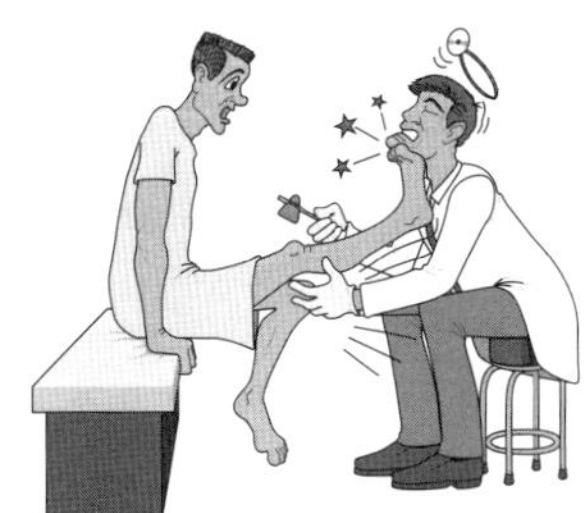

a) Reflexes happen really **fast** / **slowly**.

b) This is because you **do** / **don't** have to think about them.

c) The flow of information in a reflex is called a reflex **wave** / **arc**.

Q2 When you **touch** something **hot** you pull your hand away. This is a **reflex action**.

a) Why are reflex actions important for your body?

....

The picture on the right shows a **reflex arc** for this **reflex**.

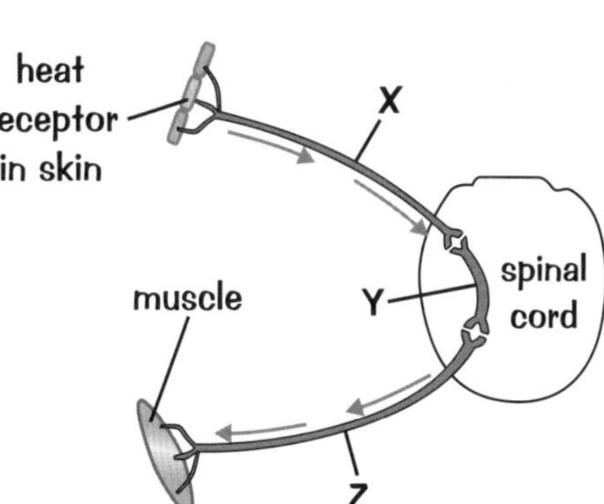

b) What type of neurone is **Y**? Circle your answer.

Sensory neurone   Relay neurone   Motor neurone

c) Circle the **effector** on the picture of the reflex arc.

Q3 John touches a **hairpin** against different bits of people's **skin**.
He asks if they can feel **both points** or **just one**. John does this to **ten people**.

Here are John's results:

Bit of skin	Number of people that could feel both points
Foot	2
Knee	3
Finger	10
Arm	5

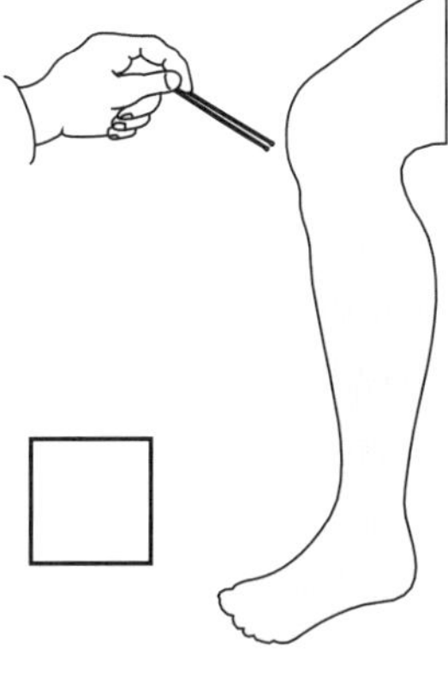

Look at the results.

a) How many people could feel both points on their **knee**?

b) Which bit of skin is the **most sensitive**?

....

c) Which bit of skin is the **least sensitive**?

....

Hormones

Q1 Tick the boxes to show if these statements are **true** or **false**.

		True	False
a)	Hormones are electrical messengers.	☐	☐
b)	Hormones are made in glands.	☐	☐
c)	Hormones are carried around the body in the blood.	☐	☐
d)	Organs that respond to hormones are called response organs.	☐	☐

Q2 The body controls your blood **sugar** level.

a) Circle **one hormone** that helps to control your blood sugar level.

insulin   oestrogen   adrenaline

b) Circle **two organs** that are involved in controlling your blood sugar level.

heart   liver   pancreas   bladder

Q3 Complete this flow chart by circling one word from each pair.

1) Eating makes the amount of glucose in the blood go **up** / **down**.

↓

2) The pancreas gives out **glucose** / **insulin**.

↓

3) This tells the liver to take glucose out of the blood. The glucose is stored as **insulin** / **glycogen**.

↓

4) The blood glucose level goes **up** / **down**.

Diabetes

Q1 Draw lines to match each type of **diabetes** to its cause.

Type 1 diabetes...	...is where the pancreas can't <u>produce</u> insulin.
Type 2 diabetes...	...is where a person can't <u>react to</u> insulin.

Q2 Joe and Jane control their diabetes by **injecting insulin** into their blood.

a) Which type of diabetes do Joe and Jane both have?

....

b) Joe gets no exercise. Jane gets lots of exercise.
Who will need to inject the **least** insulin, Joe or Jane? Circle your answer.

JOE **JANE**

Q3 Which of these can help to control **type 2 diabetes**? Circle **two** answers.

healthy diet extra sleep injecting insulin doing exercise

Q4 You can calculate someone's **body mass index** (BMI) using this formula:

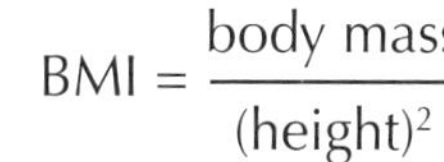

$$\text{BMI} = \frac{\text{body mass}}{(\text{height})^2}$$

a) Bob has a body mass of **128 kg** and a height of **2 m**.
Use the formula to calculate Bob's BMI.

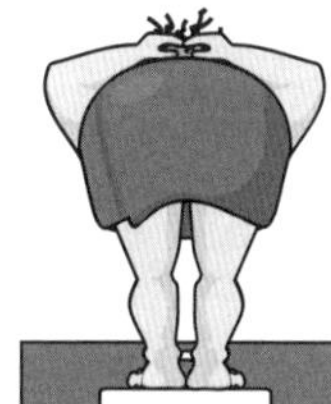

Bob's BMI is ....

b) A BMI of 30 or more means a person is obese.
Is Bob obese? Circle your answer.

Yes **No**

c) Which type of diabetes do obese people have a bigger risk of getting?

....

Plant Growth Hormones

Q1 Which of these are **plant growth hormones**? Circle **two** answers.

gibberellin insulin auxin progesterone

Q2 Draw lines to match these two terms to their meanings.

Positive phototropism	Growing towards gravity.
Positive gravitropism	Growing towards light.

Q3 Some plants are growing in a shed. Their only light comes from **three light bulbs**. Circle the **bulb** that has **broken**.

Q4 This diagram shows how **auxin** makes **shoots grow towards light**. Fill in the missing words. Choose words from the list below.

shaded grow upwards downwards bright

light

1) Auxin moves to the .... side.

light

3) The shoot bends ....

2) Auxin makes the cells there ....

Q5 Tick the boxes to show if these statements are **true** or **false**.

		True	False
a)	Auxin gathers on the upper side of roots.	☐	☐
b)	Auxin makes roots bend down (towards gravity).	☐	☐

Q6 What does **gibberellin** do? Circle **three** answers.

Makes seeds grow. Makes roots grow towards light. Makes plants flower. Makes fruit grow. Makes the stems of plants grow.

Plant Growth Hormones — Experiment

Q1 Vicky is looking at how **light** affects how cress seeds **grow**.

This diagram shows how Vicky set up her experiment:

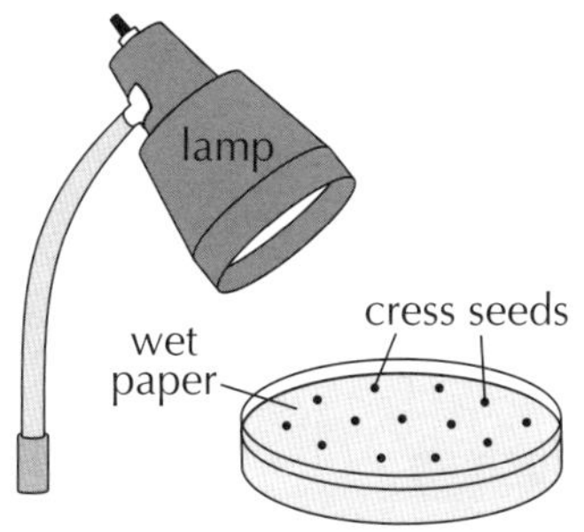

DISH 1: light from the **left**.

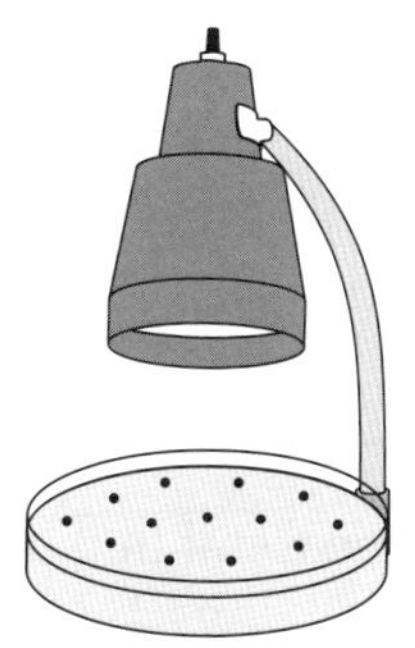

DISH 2: light from **above**.

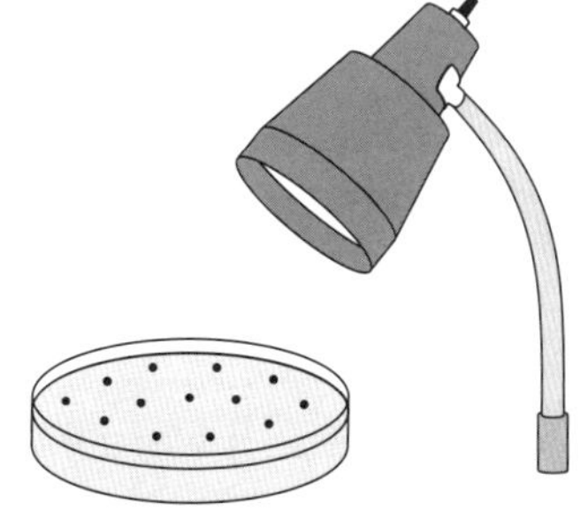

DISH 3: light from the **right**.

a) The picture below shows what the seedlings looked like after one week.
Complete the picture by **drawing** the cress seedlings on dish 3.

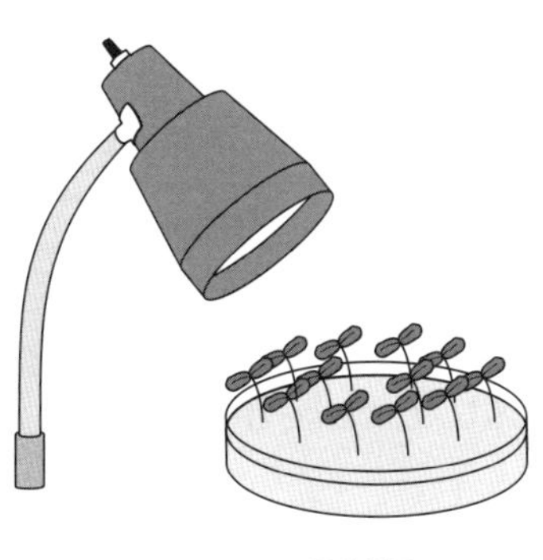

DISH 1

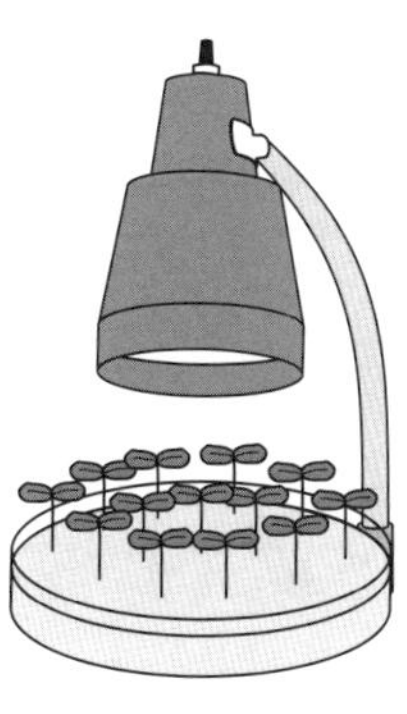

DISH 2

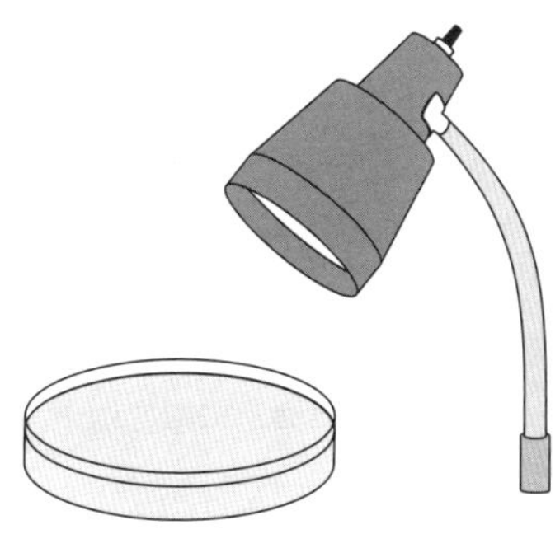

DISH 3

b) Which plant hormone made the seedlings grow towards the light?

....

c) The table below is Vicky's results table. Fill in the gaps in her table.

DISH	Light from:	Result after 1 week
1		Seedlings grew to the left.
	Above	Seedlings grew straight up.
3	Right	

d) Name **one thing** that Vicky had to keep the same in each dish to make it a fair test.

....

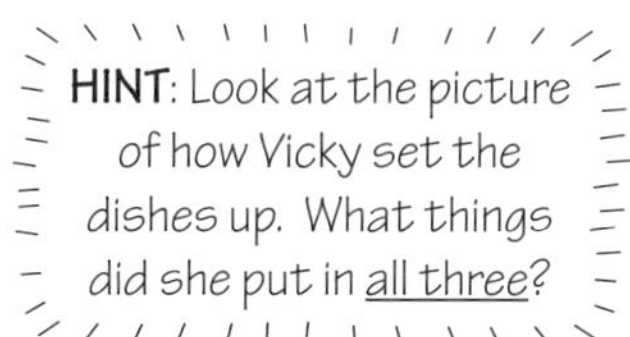

Mixed Questions — B1 Topic 2

Q1 Martin is jogging along a path. He sees a puddle in the way and **jumps over it**.

a) Which of his sense organs does Martin use to detect the puddle? Circle the answer.

tongue nose eyes ears skin

b) What is his response?

....

c) Choose a word from below the line to fill in the gap in this sentence:

The muscles that Martin uses to jump are the ....

effectors stimulus

d) Martin treads on a pin and automatically lifts his foot up.
Is this a **reflex** reaction? Tick **one** box to show your answer.

YES ☐ NO ☐

Q2 Liz eats a meal. Her **blood glucose** goes up and her body starts to make **insulin**.

a) Fill in the blanks using words from the grey box.

glycogen	liver	glucose	up	down

When Liz's blood glucose goes up, her pancreas gives out insulin. The insulin tells her .... to take glucose out of her blood. Her liver stores the glucose as .... This means that the amount of glucose in Liz's blood will go ....

b) Insulin is a hormone. How are hormones carried around the body?

....

c) Liz's Dad has type 1 diabetes. He cannot produce insulin.
How can he **control** his diabetes? Circle **two** answers.

not eating food with lots of sugar in it injecting glucose injecting insulin not doing exercise

Drugs

Q1 What is a **drug**? Tick the box next to the right sentence below.

- A chemical that is illegal. ☐
- A chemical that affects the central nervous system. ☐
- A chemical that is always harmful. ☐

Q2 Some drugs are **stimulants**.

Circle the correct words in the sentences below.

Stimulants **increase / decrease** the amount of chemicals at synapses.

Stimulants make you feel **more / less** awake.

Q3 Some drugs are **depressants**.

a) Circle the correct word in the sentence below.

Depressants **speed up / slow down** your brain.

b) Circle one drug that is a **depressant**.

morphine   caffeine   alcohol

Q4 a) Fill in the gaps in the table below.

Type of drug	Example
Stimulants	
	Morphine
Hallucinogens	

b) What do hallucinogens do?

....

Smoking, Alcohol and Organ Transplants

Q1 Draw lines to match the type of effect to what it means.

Type of Effect	What it means
short-term effects	things that happen slowly
long-term effects	things that happen quickly

Q2 Alcohol has **short-term effects**.

a) Circle **one** effect that alcohol has on **reaction time**.

speeds up reactions — slows reactions — no effect

b) Circle **one** effect that alcohol has on **vision**.

blurs vision — improves vision — no effect

c) Circle **one** effect that alcohol has on a person's **inhibitions**.

increases inhibitions — lowers inhibitions — no effect

Q3 Give two **long-term effects** of alcohol.

1. ....

2. ....

Smoking, Alcohol and Organ Transplants

Q4 Circle the correct word in the sentences below.

a) Nicotine is **infectious / addictive**.

b) Tobacco smoke has **carbon monoxide / carbon dioxide** in it.
This causes the blood to carry **more / less** oxygen.

c) The tar in tobacco smoke is a **toxin / carcinogen**.
This is a chemical that can lead to **cancer / diabetes**.

Q5 True or false? Tick the correct box.

		True	False
a)	If an organ's damaged it can be replaced by an organ from another person.	☐	☐
b)	An organ transplant can be risky for very overweight people.	☐	☐
c)	An alcoholic might not get a liver transplant unless they stop exercising.	☐	☐
d)	An organ donor is someone who gives their organs for organ transplant.	☐	☐
e)	There are enough organ donors in the UK.	☐	☐

Q6 The graph below shows how the number of **men who smoke** has changed since 1950.

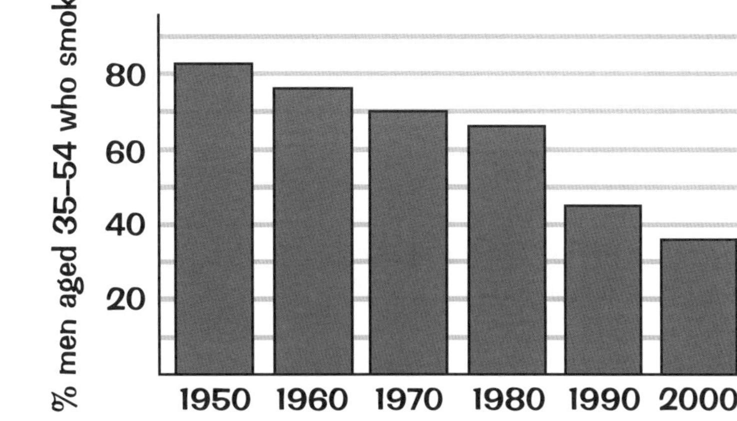

Has the number of male smokers increased, decreased or stayed the same since 1950?
Circle your answer.

increased decreased stayed the same

Infectious Diseases

Q1 True or false? Tick the correct box.

		True	False
a)	Infectious diseases are caused by pathogens.	☐	☐
b)	Infectious diseases can be passed on by genes.	☐	☐
c)	All pathogens are bacteria.	☐	☐

Q2 Circle the correct word in the sentences below.

a) Influenza is caused by a **virus / bacterium**. It is spread by **vectors / air**.

b) HIV is a **virus / bacterium**. It is passed on by **contact / body fluids**.

c) Vectors are **animals / plants** that spread disease.

Q3 Complete the table to show how different types of pathogen are spread.

How pathogen is spread:	water	food	
Example:	Cholera bacteria		Athlete's foot fungus

Q4 Draw lines to match the **vector** to the **pathogen** it carries and the **disease** it causes. An example has been done for you.

Vector	Type of pathogen it carries	Disease
mosquito	bacterium	dysentery
house fly	protozoan	typhus
lice	bacterium	malaria

Barriers to Disease

Q1 Draw lines to match the barriers to the **type** of barrier they are.

Type of Barrier

skin

CHEMICAL

lysozyme

cilia

PHYSICAL

stomach acid

Q2 Circle the type of acid in your stomach.

nitric acid

hydrochloric acid

sulfuric acid

Q3 Complete the passage below using the words in the box.

viruses eyes bacteria stomach chemical toxin

Your .... make tears.

There's a .... in tears called lysozyme.

Lysosome kills .... in your eye.

Q4 True or false? Tick the correct box.

		True	False
a)	Your skin keeps pathogens in.	☐	☐
b)	If you cut your skin, you get a scab.	☐	☐
c)	Scabs also keep pathogens in.	☐	☐

Q5 Your breathing system has **mucus** and **cilia** in it.

a) Circle the correct word in the sentence below.

Mucus catches dust and bacteria **after / before** they reach your lungs.

b) What are cilia?

....

Antiseptics and Antibiotics

Q1 Complete the passage below using the words in the box.

cause	outside	bacteria	stop	fungi	inside

Antiseptics are chemicals that kill ....

They are used .... the body.

Antiseptics .... the spread of infection.

Q2 a) What do antibiotics kill? Circle your answer.

bacteria only

bacteria and viruses

bacteria and fungi

b) Are antibiotics used inside or outside the body? Circle your answer.

inside

outside

Q3 True or false? Tick the correct box.

		True	False
a)	Pathogens don't attack plants.	☐	☐
b)	Plants can make chemicals to protect themselves.	☐	☐
c)	Some of these plant chemicals are antibacterials.	☐	☐
d)	Humans can't use these plant chemicals.	☐	☐

Q4 Antibiotics can be antibacterials or antifungals.

a) What do antibacterials kill?

....

b) What do antifungals kill?

....

Investigating Antibiotics

Q1 Put numbers in the boxes to show the order of events in **testing antibiotics**.

Soak two paper discs in different antibiotics. Soak one disc in water (this is the control). ☐

Use a loop to add bacteria to the jelly. ☐

Fill a Petri dish full of nutrient jelly. 1

Tape a lid onto the dish to stop any bacteria from the air getting in. ☐

Place the discs on the jelly. ☐

The first one has been done for you.

Bacteria
RIP

Q2 Gavin tested **two different antibiotics** to see which one worked best. His results are shown below.

Petri dish
bacteria growing
water
disc soaked in antibiotic 1
disc soaked in antibiotic 2
clear zone
1
2

a) What is the **clear zone**? Circle the answer.

where water was added   where nutrient jelly wasn't added   where bacteria can't grow

b) Circle the correct word in the sentence below.

The bigger the clear zone the **better / worse** the antibiotic.

c) Did **antibiotic 1** or **antibiotic 2** work best?

....

d) Give **one** variable that Gavin should have controlled in this experiment.

....

Energy and Biomass

Q1 Circle the correct word in the sentence below.

An organism is a living thing.

a) Biomass is how much all the organisms at each stage of a food chain **eat / weigh**.

b) Biomass is **lost / gained** at each stage of a food chain.

c) There is **less / more** biomass as you go up a food chain.

d) The size of each box in a pyramid of biomass shows the **number of organisms / amount of biomass** at that stage.

leaf it out

Q2 All living things depend on each other for things like food.

What is this called? Circle your answer.

interdependence **dependence** **photosynthesis**

Q3 True or false? Tick the correct box.

	True	False
a) Plants use the Sun's energy to make food.	☐	☐
b) Energy is gained at each stage of a food chain.	☐	☐
c) Energy is lost from the food chain as heat.	☐	☐
d) The size of a food chain is limited by the amount of sunlight lost from plants.	☐	☐

Q4 The **pyramid of biomass** below shows a seashore food chain.

crab
winkle
algae

a) Which organism eats the winkles?

....

b) Which organism has the biggest biomass?

....

c) Which organism has the smallest biomass?

....

Parasites and Mutualism

Q1 True or false? Tick the correct box.

	True	False
a) A parasite is an organism that uses another organism to live.	☐	☐
b) Parasites live in or on a host.	☐	☐
c) Parasites give their hosts things they need to survive.	☐	☐
d) Parasites can't cause harm.	☐	☐

Q2 What happens in mutualism? Tick the correct box.

☐ one organism gains something and the other isn't harmed

☐ one organism gains something and the other is harmed

☐ both organisms gain something

Q3 Draw a line to match each **parasite** with its description.

Mistletoe	They live in the fur of animals. They suck blood for food.
Tapeworms	They live on human heads. They suck blood for food.
Fleas	They stick to the gut walls of their hosts. They take lots of nutrients.
Head lice	It grows on trees. It takes water and food from its host.

Q4 Oxpeckers are birds. They live on the backs of buffalo.

a) What do oxpeckers get from the buffalo? Circle your answer.

cleaned   food   air

b) What do the buffalo get from the oxpeckers?

....

Human Activity and Recycling

Q1 Circle the correct word in the sentence below.

Recycling something means it's not **used again** / **thrown away**.

Q2 Circle **three advantages** of recycling.

less landfill

more energy and material are used

more landfill

less energy and materials are used

less toxic waste is made

Q3 True or false? Tick the correct box.

		True	False
a)	We get metals from rocks called ores.	☐	☐
b)	Getting metal out of rocks doesn't use a lot of energy.	☐	☐
c)	Paper is made from wood.	☐	☐
d)	Recycling paper uses more energy than making new paper.	☐	☐

Q4 Circle the correct word in the sentence below.

a) Plastic is made from **metal** / **oil**.

b) Plastic rots very **quickly** / **slowly**.

c) Recycling plastic means **less** / **more** landfill.

Q5 Draw lines to match each material to an advantage of recycling it.

Material	Advantage of recycling
PLASTIC	fewer trees are cut down
METAL	oil is saved
PAPER	it doesn't use up ores

Human Activity and Recycling

Q6 Human activity can add **pollutants** to the environment.
Give an **example** of what each pollutant below is used in.

Pollutant: **Nitrates**

Example: ....

Pollutant: **Phosphates**

Example: ....

Pollutant: **Sulfur dioxide**

Example: ....

Q7 The graph below shows how the world's population has changed since 1000.

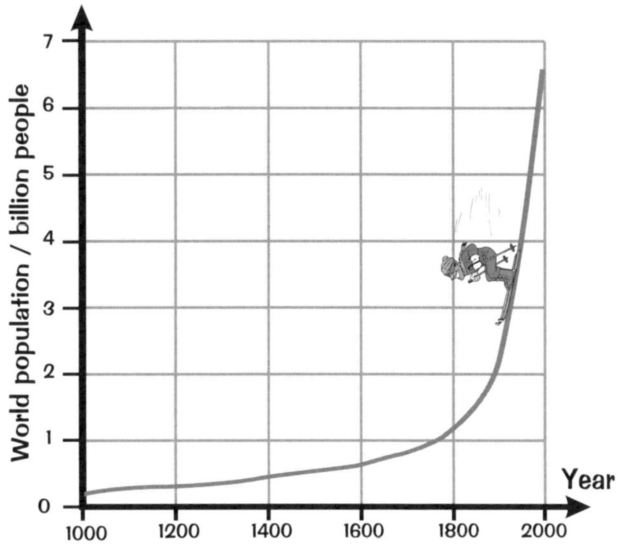

a) How has the world's population changed? Tick the answer.

The world's population has increased at the same rate between the year 1000 and 2000.	☐
The world's population increased slowly until 1800. It then increased very quickly.	☐
The world's population increased quickly until 1800. It then increased very slowly.	☐

b) Is human population growth causing **more** or **less** pollution?

....

Pollutants and Plant Growth

Q1 Rivers and lakes can be **polluted** by **fertilisers**.

a) Number these sentences in the correct order. The **first** one has been done for you.

The bacteria use up all the oxygen in the water. All the animals in the water die. ☐

The amount of bacteria increases. ☐

Fertilisers with nitrates in them get into a river. **1**

The nitrates make algae grow fast. The algae stop sunlight from getting to the plants. ☐

Plants start dying. They're eaten by bacteria. ☐

b) What is this type of pollution called?

....

Q2 A student put **seeds** in four different dishes. Each dish had a **different concentration** (amount) of nitrate in it. The results are shown below.

A: no nitrate

C: high nitrate concentration

B: low nitrate concentration

D: very high nitrate concentration

a) In which dish did the plants grow **best**?

....

b) In which dish did the plants grow **worst**?

....

c) What **concentration** of nitrates is **best** for plant growth?

....

Indicator Species

Q1 The pictures below show two rivers.

RIVER A

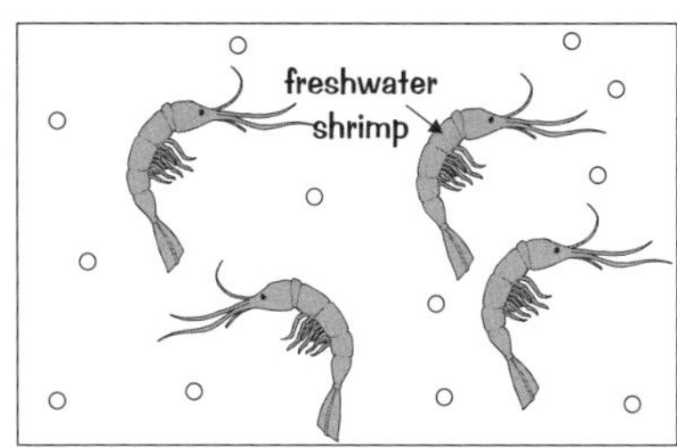

RIVER B

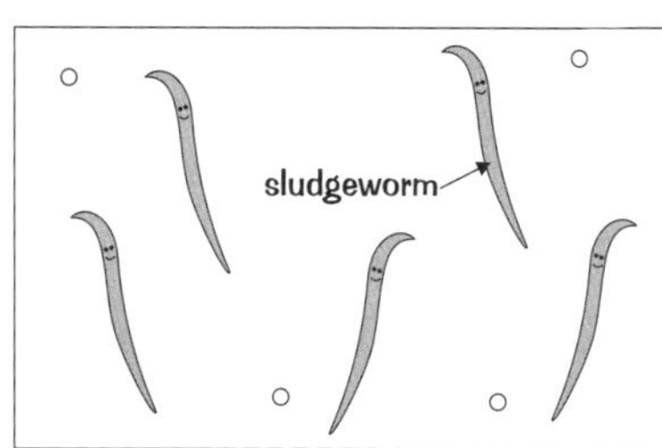

a) Which river is polluted? Tick the right box.

☐ **RIVER A** ☐ **RIVER B**

b) How can you tell this river is polluted?

....

Q2 True or false? Tick the correct box.

		True	False
a)	Blackspot fungus can't live where there is a lot of sulfur dioxide.	☐	☐
b)	Bloodworms live in water with lots of oxygen.	☐	☐
c)	If you find bloodworms in a river, the water is clean.	☐	☐
d)	Blackspot fungus is a fungus on plants.	☐	☐

Q3 The graph below shows the **number of lichen** found in different areas.

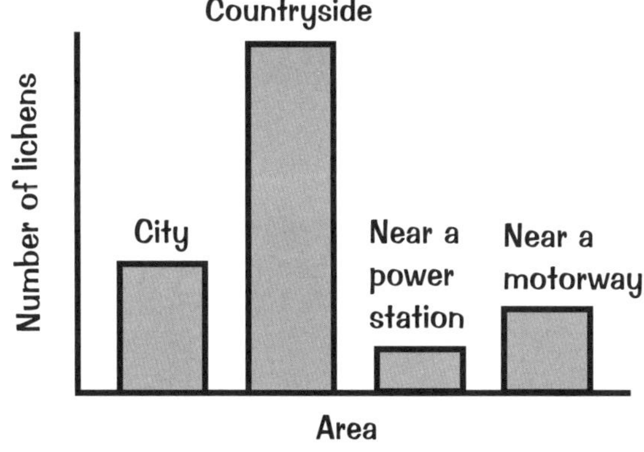

a) Where are the most lichen found? Circle your answer.

city countryside near a power station near a motorway

b) If you find lots of lichen the air is ....

clean polluted

The Carbon Cycle

Q1 Complete the passage below using the words in the box.

combustion	respiration	photosynthesis

Plants take carbon dioxide out of the air during ....

Animals and plants release carbon dioxide into the air during ....

Fossil fuels release carbon dioxide into the air during ....

Q2 Put numbers in the boxes below to match the arrows to the correct words.

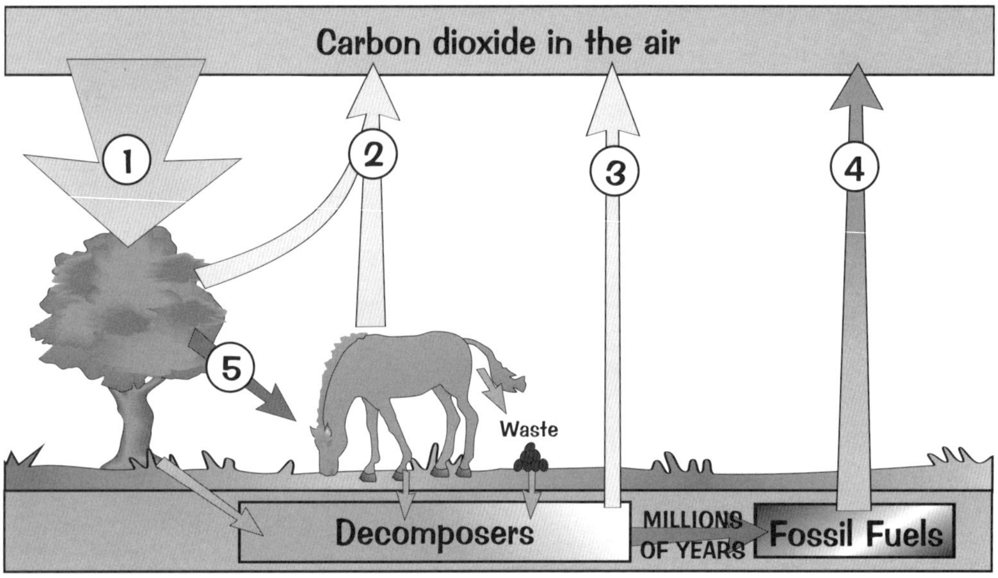

☐ respiration (by decomposers) ☐ combustion ☐ photosynthesis

☐ eating ☐ respiration (by plants and animals)

Q3 True or false? Tick the correct box.

		True	False
a)	The carbon in plants goes into animals that eat them.	☐	☐
b)	Decomposers break down dead organisms.	☐	☐
c)	Decomposers don't break down waste.	☐	☐
d)	Carbon dioxide is released when fossil fuels are burnt.	☐	☐

Mixed Questions — B1 Topic 3

Q1 The diagram below shows a **food chain**.

grass → gazelle → cheetah

a) Where does the grass get its energy from?

....

b) Tick two ways that energy might be lost by the gazelle.

- [ ] heat loss
- [ ] photosynthesis
- [ ] building biomass
- [ ] waste materials

c) Tick one way that energy might be used by the gazelle.

- [ ] movement
- [ ] combustion
- [ ] eutrophication

d) How does carbon pass from the grass to the gazelle? Circle your answer.

respiration **movement** **eating**

Q2 **Pathogens** can get into our bodies.

a) Circle **two** pathogens.

HIV virus house fly Cholera bacteria fleas

b) Your tears have a chemical in them to kill bacteria. What is it called?

....

c) Your stomach has a chemical in it to kill pathogens. What is it called?

....

The Early Atmosphere

Q1 Tick the box next to **one** sentence below that is **true**.

The atmosphere today is mostly argon. ☐
The atmosphere today is mostly oxygen. ☐
The atmosphere today contains nitrogen. ☐

Q2 The amount of **carbon dioxide** in the atmosphere has changed.

a) Circle the correct word in the sentence below.

There is **more / less** carbon dioxide in the atmosphere now than billions of years ago.

b) Some carbon dioxide has become part of rocks.
What name is given to these rocks? Circle your answer.

carbonate rocks **carbon dioxide rocks** **igneous rocks**

Q3 Draw lines to put the statements in the **right order** on the timeline. One has been done for you.

A very long time ago

Water vapour turned to water to make the oceans.

Volcanoes gave out a lot of carbon dioxide and some water vapour.

A lot of the carbon dioxide dissolved in the oceans. Plants took in carbon dioxide too.

Now

The Early Atmosphere

Q4 a) This pie chart shows the amounts of different gases in the **Earth's atmosphere today**.

Add these labels to the pie chart:

Nitrogen **Oxygen** **Argon**

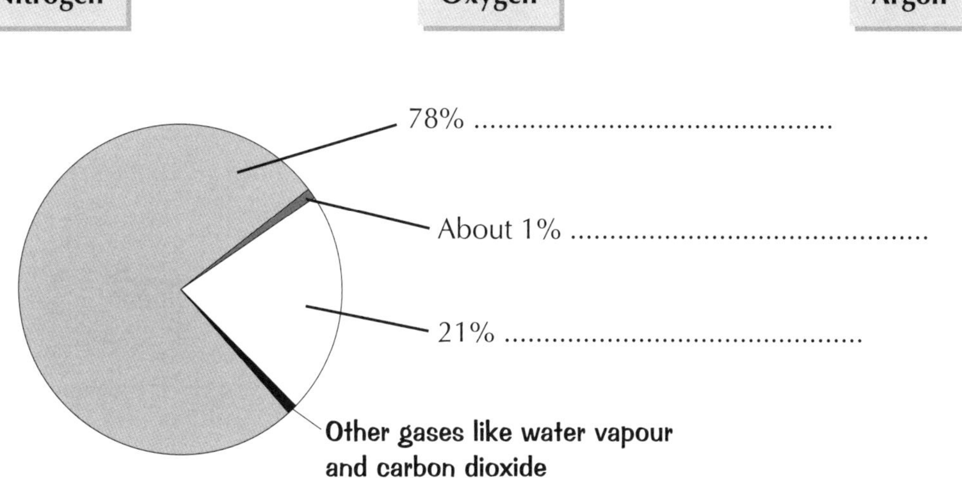

b) Billions of years ago there was **a lot more carbon dioxide** in the atmosphere. Tick the box next to **one** thing that has made the amount of carbon dioxide change.

☐ Sea creatures took it in

☐ Volcanoes took it in

☐ Burning fossil fuels got rid of it

c) What made the amount of water vapour in the atmosphere change? Tick the answer.

Sea creatures took in the water vapour. ☐

Plants took in the water vapour for photosynthesis. ☐

Water vapour turned to water to make the oceans. ☐

d) What gives out oxygen? Circle your answer.

rocks plants

sea water volcanoes

Today's Atmosphere

Q1 The amount of **carbon dioxide** in the atmosphere is still changing. The graph shows this change.

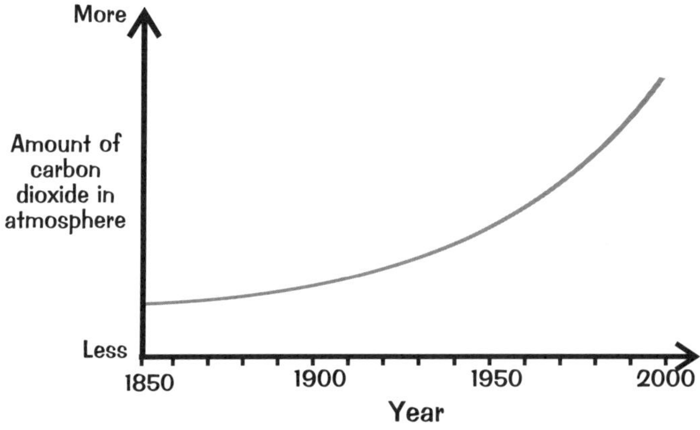

a) Has the amount of carbon dioxide in the atmosphere increased or decreased since 1850? Circle your answer.

increased   decreased

b) Which of these change the amount of carbon dioxide in the air? Circle **three** answers.

volcanoes   acid rain   deforestation   burning fossil fuels

c) Circle the correct word in the sentence below.

A human activity that changes the atmosphere is **erosion** / **farming**.

Q2 Mr Jones does an experiment to work out the **percentage of oxygen** in air. He does the experiment **twice** and writes down his results in a table.

Experiment number	**1**	**2**
Percentage of oxygen in air	20.6%	21.0%

What is the **average** percentage of oxygen from the two experiments? Circle your answer.

20.8%   83.2%   0.4%   41.6%

Work out the average by adding the two percentages together and dividing by two.

The Three Different Types of Rock

Q1 Join up each **rock type** with how it's **made** and an **example**.

ROCK TYPE	HOW IT'S MADE	EXAMPLE
metamorphic rock	made from layers of sediment	limestone
sedimentary rock	made from other rocks by heat and pressure	marble

Q2 The diagrams below show the **crystals** in two types of igneous rock.

Draw lines to match each rock with how quickly it cooled.

The size of the crystals tells you how quickly the rock cooled.

crystal

cooled quickly

cooled slowly

Q3 Erica has found **fossils** in the walls of a church.

Which type of rock is the church likely to be built from? Circle your answer.

igneous sedimentary metamorphic

Q4 Sedimentary rock is made when sediment is **squeezed**.

a) Which one of these is a type of sedimentary rock? Circle your answer.

granite marble chalk

b) What is it called when a layer of sediment is squeezed by the layers above?

....

The Three Different Types of Rock

Q5 The diagram below shows **metamorphic** rock being made.

a) Add these labels to the diagram:

Heat from below

Metamorphic rock made here

Pressure from rocks above

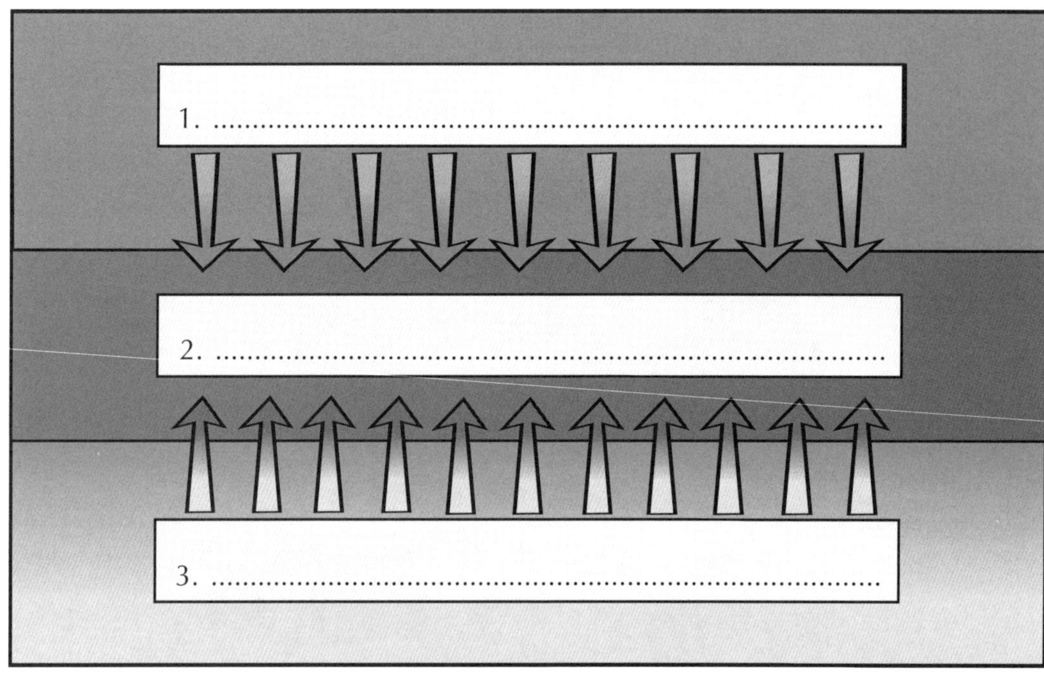

b) Which of these rocks may be made into metamorphic rock? Circle **two** answers.

marble limestone chalk granite

Q6 True or false? Tick the correct box.

		True	False
a)	Sedimentary rocks are made in a few seconds.	☐	☐
b)	Chalk is a metamorphic rock.	☐	☐
c)	Limestone can be made into a different type of rock.	☐	☐
d)	Sedimentary rocks are eroded easily.	☐	☐
e)	Fossils are found in lava.	☐	☐

Using Limestone

Q1 a) Circle **one disadvantage** of quarrying.

Waste from quarries is messy and ugly

Quarries cost the country a lot of money

Quarries cause fires

b) Circle **two** advantages of quarrying.

Quarries are quiet

There are jobs at the quarry

Quarries make a lot of money

Quarries are good homes for birds and animals

Tourists like to visit quarries

Q2 Burt is a builder. Look at his shopping list below.
Tick the materials that are made using **limestone**.

Cement	☐	Glass	☐
Wood	☐	Plastic	☐
Concrete	☐	Copper	☐

Q3 What is **limestone** mainly made of? Circle your answer.

sodium carbonate   calcium hydroxide   calcium carbonate

Q4 Some power stations give off **acidic gases**.

Limestone can be used to get rid of these acidic gases. What problem does this help to stop?

....

Q5 Fill in the gap in the sentence using one of the words below.

make   neutralise   quarry   oxidise

Calcium carbonate is used to .... acid soil.

Limestone and Thermal Decomposition

Q1 a) Name the **two** products made when calcium carbonate is heated.

1. ....

2. ....

b) What has happened to the carbonate? Tick the correct answer.

It has been neutralised. ☐

It has been thermally decomposed. ☐

It has been cracked. ☐

Q2 Calcium oxide can make **calcium hydroxide**.

a) Fill in the gap in the equation using one of the options below.

oxygen carbon dioxide water

calcium oxide + ... → calcium hydroxide

b) What can calcium hydroxide do to acidic soil? Circle your answer.

make it more acidic turn it into limestone make it neutral

Q3 Below is a list of three **metal carbonates**. They are in order of least stable to most stable.

magnesium carbonate	Least stable
calcium carbonate	↓
barium carbonate	Most stable

Which carbonate would break down **most easily**? Circle your answer.

magnesium carbonate calcium carbonate barium carbonate

Q4 **Copper carbonate** can be thermally decomposed. Circle the **two** products that are made.

copper oxide copper chloride water

oxygen carbon dioxide

Atoms and Mass in Chemical Reactions

Q1 Use the words below to fill in the blanks in the passage.

chemical	compounds	physical	particles

Atoms are the tiny .... that make up everything.

Atoms take part in .... reactions.

Q2 Draw lines to match the word to its meaning.

Products	The stuff that reacts
Reactants	The stuff that is made

Q3 Circle the correct words in the sentences below.

During a reaction the number of atoms **stays the same** / **changes**.

The properties of the products are **different to** / **the same as** the properties of the reactants.

Properties are things like how hard something is or what colour it is.

Q4 Fill in the gaps on the scales to show the mass of the chemicals.

a)

REACTANTS PRODUCT

b)

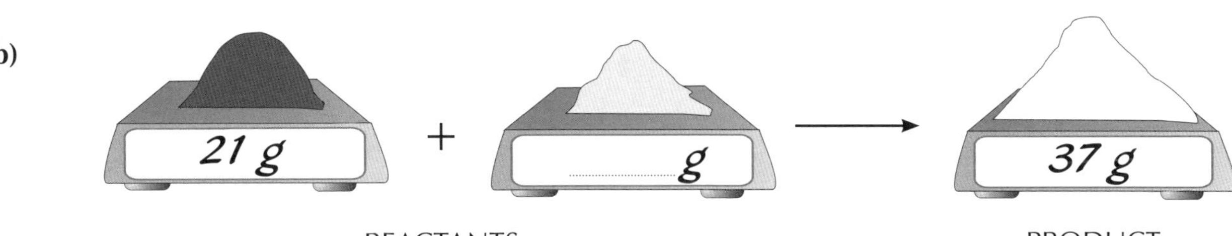

REACTANTS PRODUCT

Mixed Questions — C1a Topics 1 & 2

Q1 Use **one** of the options from the boxes to complete the two equations.

a)

heat	water	electricity

calcium carbonate —— + ... ——→ calcium oxide + carbon dioxide

b)

calcium hydroxide	carbon dioxide	calcium carbonate

calcium oxide + water ——→ ....

c) Tick **three** uses of limestone.

- Getting rid of acidic gases in power stations. ☐
- Making plastics. ☐
- Making cement. ☐
- Making acidic soils neutral. ☐
- Testing for carbon dioxide. ☐

d) Circle **two** problems with quarrying for limestone.

Destroys the homes of animals and birds

Sets off volcanoes

Makes people ill

Makes noise and pollution from lorries

Q2 a) Limestone can be turned into **marble**.

What type of rock is marble? Circle the correct word.

sedimentary metamorphic igneous

b) Tick the box that says how limestone is turned into marble.

☐ Heat and pressure change limestone into marble over a long time.

☐ Limestone cools and becomes solid.

☐ Layers of limestone are squeezed over time.

Mixed Questions — C1a Topics 1 & 2

Q3 The graphs give information about the Earth's atmosphere billions of years ago and today.

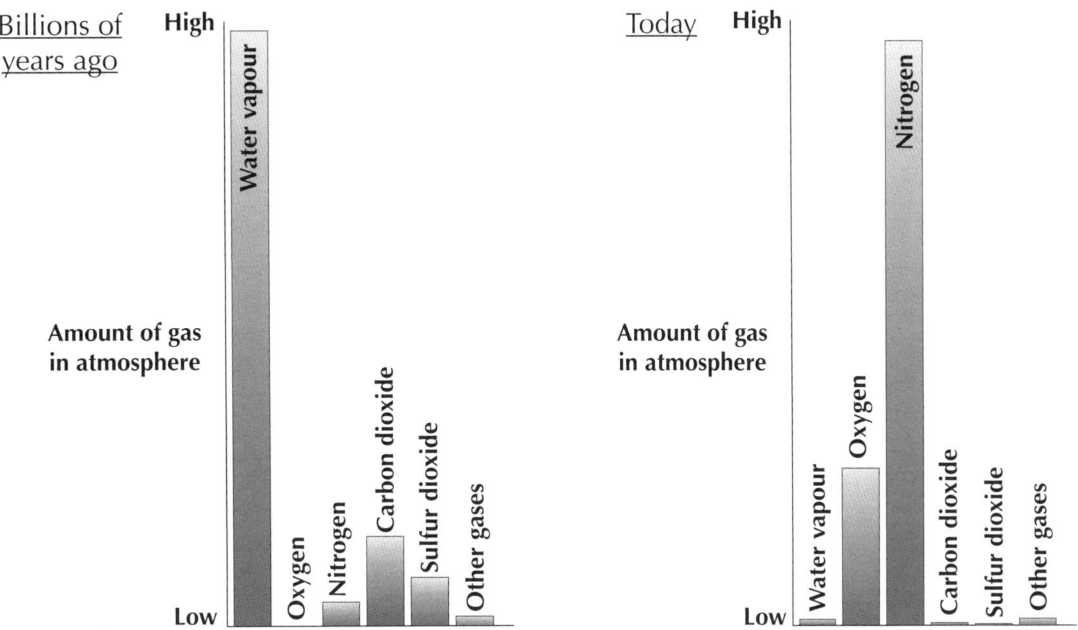

a) Look at the graphs. What has happened to the amount of nitrogen in the atmosphere?

....

b) Tick **two** boxes to show which sentences are true.

A small amount of the atmosphere today is argon.	☐
Volcanoes give out carbon dioxide.	☐
Farm animals take in methane.	☐
80% of the atmosphere today is water vapour.	☐

Q4 **Deforestation** and **burning fossil fuels** can change the atmosphere.

a) What is deforestation?

....

b) Circle the correct words in the sentences below.

Burning fossil fuels **increases** / **decreases** the amount of carbon dioxide in the atmosphere.

Deforestation **reduces** / **increases** the amount of carbon dioxide in the atmosphere.

Mixed Questions — C1a Topics 1 & 2

Q5 Fill in the gaps to show if the sentence is talking about **sedimentary**, **metamorphic** or **igneous** rock.

One has been done for you.

TYPE OF ROCK

This rock is made by compaction of sediment layers. ....sedimentary.........

a) Marble is this type of rock. ....

b) This type of rock is made from lava. ....

c) Granite is this type of rock. ....

d) This type of rock can be eroded easily. ....

Q6 **Carbon** and **oxygen** react together to make a molecule of carbon dioxide.

carbon + oxygen → carbon dioxide

a) How many atoms of carbon were there at the start of the reaction? ....

b) How many atoms of oxygen were there at the start of the reaction? ....

c) Circle the right word in the sentence below.

Atoms **are / aren't** made or lost in a chemical reaction.

Q7 a) What happens to the **mass** of reactants and products during a reaction? Tick the box next to your answer.

The mass of the reactants is the same as the mass of the products. ☐

The mass of the reactants is larger than the mass of the products. ☐

The mass of the reactants is smaller than the mass of the products. ☐

b) **12 g** of a chemical reacts with **15 g** of another chemical.
What would the total mass of the **products** be? Circle your answer.

27 g 3 g 30 g

Hazard Symbols, Acids and Alkalis

Q1 What are **hazard symbols**? Tick the box next to the answer.

Hazard symbols tell you the name of the chemical. ☐

Hazard symbols tell you how much of the chemical to use. ☐

Hazard symbols tell you how a chemical is dangerous. ☐

Hazard symbols tell you if a chemical is neutral. ☐

Q2 Circle the right words in the sentences below.

a) The **pH** / **indicator** number of a chemical tells you if it's an acid, an alkali or neutral.

b) A chemical with a pH of 7 is **acidic** / **neutral**.

c) The pH number of an alkali is **more** / **less** than 7.

Q3 Here is a list of **chemicals** and their **pH numbers**.

Fill in the gap for each chemical by writing if it's an **acid**, an **alkali** or **neutral**.

	pH NUMBER	ACID, ALKALI OR NEUTRAL
a) Lemon juice	4	....
b) Pure water	7	....
c) Soap	11	....
d) Vinegar	3	....
e) Baking soda	9	....

Stomach Acid and Indigestion Tablets

Q1 Circle the right words in the sentences below.

The stomach makes acid to help **digest / smell** food.

Having acid in the stomach also helps to **make / kill** bacteria.

Indigestion is caused by having **too little / too much** acid in the stomach.

Indigestion tablets have an **acid / alkali** in them.

Indigestion tablets **neutralise the acid / make the acid stronger**.

Q2 Joey is testing **different indigestion tablets**. He wants to find the **best** one.

a) Number the boxes to put his method in the correct order. The first one has been done for you.

☐ Work out how much acid is used.

☐ Slowly add acid. Stop when the indicator changes colour.

1 Dissolve the tablet in water.

☐ Add an indicator.

b) The table shows how much acid was needed to neutralise each tablet.

Tablet	Volume of acid needed / cm^3
A	15.0
B	17.5
C	21.0

Which tablet is the best? Circle your answer.

Tablet A **Tablet B** **Tablet C**

c) How can you tell that this tablet is the best?

....

Reactions of Acids

Q1 Fill in the gaps in the sentences below using the words in the boxes.

sulfate | nitrate | chloride

a) Hydrochloric acid always gives .... salts.

b) Sulfuric acid always gives .... salts.

c) Nitric acid always gives .... salts.

Q2 Complete the **general word equation** below.

acid + metal hydroxide → salt + ...

Q3 Draw lines to match the reaction to the salt that's made.

REACTION	SALT
hydrochloric acid + copper oxide	potassium nitrate
nitric acid + potassium hydroxide	copper chloride

Q4 Barry is looking at a chemical reaction between an acid and a metal carbonate.

sulfuric acid + sodium carbonate

Are the following sentences true or false?

		True	False
a)	A salt called a chloride is made in the reaction.	☐	☐
b)	Sodium sulfate is made in the reaction.	☐	☐
c)	Carbon dioxide is made in the reaction.	☐	☐
d)	Water is not made in the reaction.	☐	☐

Electrolysis

Q1 Circle the right words in the sentences below.

Electrolysis uses **heat** / **electricity**.

This comes from a **d.c.** / **a.c.** supply.

Q2 Tick the box next to the sentence that is true.

- Gases are tested using electrolysis. ☐
- Compounds can be broken down using electrolysis. ☐
- Gases can be broken down using electrolysis. ☐
- Water is always made during electrolysis. ☐

Q3 **Chlorine gas and hydrogen** gas can be made by electrolysis.

a) What is broken down to make hydrogen and chlorine gas? Circle your answer.

water dilute hydrochloric acid oxygen

b) You can test for hydrogen and chlorine. Draw lines to match the gases to the test you'd use. Then draw lines to show what happens in each test.

GAS	TEST	WHAT HAPPENS
chlorine	damp litmus paper	squeaky pop
hydrogen	lighted splint	bleaches the paper

Electrolysis

Q4 a) **Sea water** is mainly **salt** dissolved in water. What is the salt? Circle your answer.

sodium hydroxide **sodium nitrate** **sodium chloride**

b) What is the name of a gas made during the electrolysis of sea water? Circle your answer.

carbon dioxide **chlorine** **oxygen**

The pie chart shows what the gas is used for.

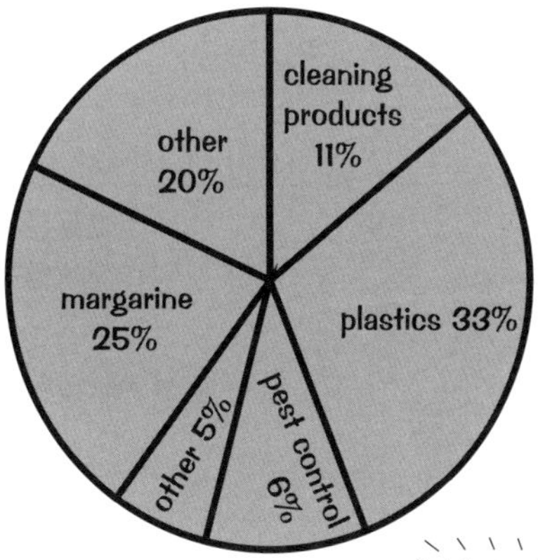

Hint: this will have the biggest section on the pie chart.

c) What is the gas used for the **most**?

....

Q5 Are these sentences true or false? Tick the boxes.

		True	False
a)	The electrolysis of sea water makes chlorine.	☐	☐
b)	Chlorine gas is toxic.	☐	☐
c)	Chlorine can be used to make bleach.	☐	☐
d)	Chlorine cannot be used to make PVC.	☐	☐

Q6 **Water** can be broken down by electrolysis. **Two** gases are made.

a) Hydrogen is one of the gases made. What is the name of the **other gas**?

....

b) You can test for this gas using a **glowing splint**. What would you **see** if the gas was there?

....

Metal Ores

Q1 Circle the correct word in each pair below.

Some metals can be found on their own in the ground. These metals are **reactive** / **unreactive**.

Other metals react with other things in the ground to form **ores** / **carbon**.

These are found in the Earth's **core** / **crust**.

A **metal** / **salt** can be removed from these.

Q2 Draw lines to match up the **process** with what it means.

PROCESS	WHAT IT MEANS
Reduction	Loss of oxygen
Oxidation	Gain of oxygen

Q3 Circle the word to complete these sentences.

a) Carbon can be used to extract metals **above** / **below** it in the reactivity series.

b) Metals below carbon in the reactivity series are **more** / **less** reactive than carbon.

Q4 Tick the boxes below to show which metals **can't** be extracted using carbon.

Use the reactivity series to help you.

The Reactivity Series
Potassium
Calcium
Magnesium
CARBON
Zinc
Tin
Copper

Metal	
Potassium	☐
Copper	☐
Tin	☐
Calcium	☐
Magnesium	☐
Zinc	☐

Q5 This reaction uses carbon to extract a metal from its ore:

copper oxide + carbon → copper + carbon dioxide

a) In this reaction, what is the ore? Circle your answer.

copper oxide   carbon   copper   carbon dioxide

b) In this reaction, what metal is extracted? Circle your answer.

copper oxide   carbon   copper   carbon dioxide

Reduction of Metal Ores

Q1 Circle the words to compete these sentences.

Electrolysis / Reduction is the breakdown of a substance using electricity.

Electrolysis **can / cannot** be used to extract metals from their ore.

Q2 Tick the boxes to show if the sentences are **true** or **false**.

	True	False
a) Aluminium is above carbon in the reactivity series.	☐	☐
b) Aluminium can be extracted by electrolysis.	☐	☐
c) Iron can only be extracted using electrolysis.	☐	☐

Q3 **Carbon** is used to extract **iron** from its ore.

a) Fill in the gaps in the equation using the words below.

iron **iron oxide**

Iron oxide is an ore of iron.

.... + carbon → .... + carbon dioxide

b) What is done to the iron oxide during this reaction? Circle your answer.

it is cooled **it is oxidised** **it is heated**

c) What name is given to this type of reaction? Circle your answer.

oxidation **reduction** **neutralisation**

d) Why is iron extracted using carbon? Tick the correct box.

Extracting iron using carbon doesn't make carbon dioxide.	☐
Iron is below carbon in the reactivity series.	☐
Pure copper is also made during the reaction.	☐
Iron is above carbon in the reactivity series.	☐

Properties of Metals

Q1 Use the words below to **complete** this passage about corrosion.

> Corrosion is the **making / breaking down** of a metal.
>
> Corrosion happens because a metal is **reduced / oxidised**.
>
> Metals which are high in the reactivity series are **more / less** likely to corrode.

Q2 Circle the **property** that makes the metal good for its use.

a) Aluminium is used to make **aircraft**.

conducts electricity shiny light conducts heat

b) Copper is used to make the **bases** of saucepans and frying pans.

conducts electricity shiny light conducts heat

c) Gold is used to make **jewellery**.

conducts electricity shiny light conducts heat

d) Copper is used for **electrical cables**.

conducts electricity shiny light conducts heat

Q3 Nicky is choosing between **aluminium** and **iron** to make window frames.

ALUMINIUM	IRON
1) Very light	1) Very heavy
2) Doesn't corrode easily	2) Corrodes easily

a) Which metal should Nicky use? Circle your answer.

aluminium iron

b) Give **one** reason for your choice.

....

Making Metals More Useful

Q1 Tick the boxes to show if the sentences are **true** or **false**.

		True	False
a)	An alloy is a metal that has been mixed with other things.	☐	☐
b)	Alloys are only made up of metal atoms.	☐	☐
c)	Alloys always have oxygen in them.	☐	☐
d)	Alloys are always weaker than pure metals.	☐	☐

Q2 Iron can be made into a **steel** alloy.

Circle the correct words in the sentences below.

a) Steel alloys are made from iron by **adding / removing** carbon.

b) Pure iron can be made **softer / harder** by adding carbon to it.

ALLOYS

Q3 The diagrams below show the **atoms** in two substances, A and B.

A

B

KEY:
= iron atoms
= carbon atoms

a) Draw lines to match the name of the diagram to the name of the substance.

DIAGRAM	SUBSTANCE
diagram A	iron
diagram B	steel

b) Which is more likely to **corrode**? Circle your answer.

A B

c) Which is **stronger**? Circle your answer.

A B

Recycling

Q1 Tick the boxes to show if the sentences are **true** or **false**.

		True	False
a)	It is important to recycle metal because there is a fixed amount of metal in the Earth.	☐	☐
b)	Recycling metals causes more pollution than mining metals.	☐	☐
c)	Recycling metals isn't good for the environment.	☐	☐

Q2 Which of the following are **good reasons** for recycling metals? Tick **two** boxes.

- ☐ Recycled metals are much shinier.
- ☐ It can use less energy and less fossil fuels.
- ☐ It can save money.
- ☐ Recycling metals is less noisy than mining.

Q3 Amelie has made a list of the **advantages** and **disadvantages** of recycling metals.

Fill in the table to show which are advantages and which are disadvantages.

One has been done for you.

Machines used to sort the waste use lots of energy.
Recycling means we mine less metal.
It costs money to collect the waste.
Lorries used to move the waste cause pollution.
Recycling means less rubbish in rubbish tips.
~~There are jobs at the recycling plant.~~

ADVANTAGES OF RECYCLING ✓	DISADVANTAGES OF RECYCLING ✗
There are jobs at the recycling plant.	

Fractional Distillation of Crude Oil

Q1 Tick the box to show which two elements **hydrocarbons** are made of.

carbon and hydrogen ☐ chlorine and hydrogen ☐ carbon and oxygen ☐

Q2 Circle the word to complete these sentences.

a) Crude oil is a **mixture** / **compound** of different substances.

b) Crude oil has **carbohydrates** / **hydrocarbons** in it

c) Fractions are made of molecules of **similar** / **different** sizes.

d) The fractions from crude oil are **renewable** / **non-renewable**.

Q3 Draw lines to match up each crude oil **fraction** to its use.

Gases	Surface for roads and roofs
Petrol	Fuel for lorries, trains and some cars
Kerosene	Aircraft fuel
Diesel Oil	Cooking and heating
Fuel Oil	Fuel for cars
Bitumen	Fuel for ships and some power stations

Q4 Different **length** hydrocarbons have different **properties**. Fill in the table using the properties from the box below.

One has been done for you.

high boiling point ~~runny~~ viscous hard to set on fire flammable low boiling point

LONG HYDROCARBON	SHORT HYDROCARBON
	runny

Burning Fuels

Q1 a) Circle the word below that means 'burning'.

combustion | neutralisation | thermal decomposition

b) Below is the equation for burning a hydrocarbon. Fill in the gaps to complete the equation.

hydrocarbon + oxygen → .... + ...

c) Complete the sentence below by circling the correct words.

When a hydrocarbon is burnt, the carbon and hydrogen are **oxidised / reduced.**

Q2 When fuels burn there isn't always enough **oxygen**.

a) Match the **amount of oxygen** to the **gas given off** and the **type of burning**.
Draw lines between the boxes.

Amount of oxygen	Gas given off	Type of burning
plenty of oxygen	carbon monoxide	complete combustion
not enough oxygen	carbon dioxide	incomplete combustion

b) Why is carbon monoxide bad? Circle your answer.

It causes acid rain. | It is toxic. | It dissolves metal.

Q3 Some fuels are **better** than other fuels.

Tick three things you should think about when choosing a fuel to use.

- How much heat energy it gives out. ☐
- How much water it makes. ☐
- How easily it burns. ☐
- If it's easy to store or transport. ☐
- The amount of oxygen it'll use to burn. ☐

Environmental Problems

Q1 Circle the words to finish the sentences below.

Power stations and cars burn **fossil fuels / nitrogen**.

But, some hydrocarbon fuels contain **impurities / acid rain**.

An impurity in some fossil fuels is **sulfur / sulfur dioxide**.

When they are burnt this is put into the air as **sulfur / sulfur dioxide**.

Q2 a) Which of the following sentences is **true**? Tick **one** box.

- Sulfur dioxide causes acid rain. ☐
- Acid rain reacts with sulfur dioxide. ☐
- Acid rain makes sulfur dioxide. ☐
- All clouds make acid rain. ☐
- Acid rain is when drops of sulfur fall from clouds. ☐

b) Circle **two** problems that acid rain causes.

- kills trees
- makes lakes unsafe for swimming
- causes volcanoes
- damages limestone buildings and statues

c) Give one other problem caused by acid rain.

....

More Environmental Problems

Q1 Which of the following sentences are **true**? Tick **two** boxes.

- [ ] Carbon dioxide is a greenhouse gas.
- [ ] Greenhouse gases don't help to keep the Earth warm.
- [ ] Human activity isn't changing the amount of carbon dioxide in the atmosphere.
- [ ] Gases like carbon dioxide send heat back to the Earth.

Q2 Look at the graph and then answer the questions below.

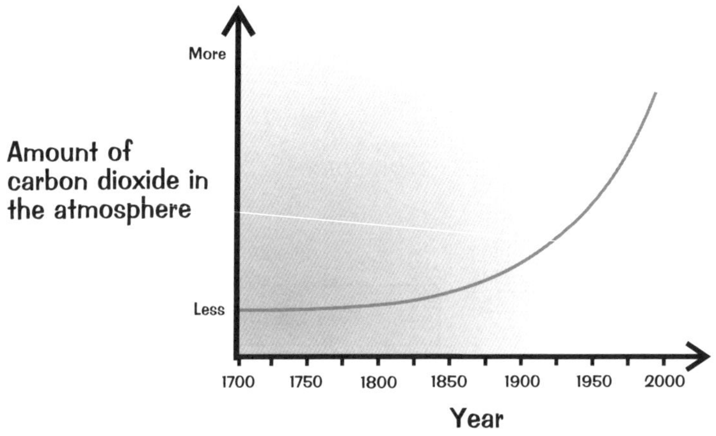

Amount of carbon dioxide in the atmosphere

More

Less

1700 1750 1800 1850 1900 1950 2000

Year

a) What has happened to the amount of carbon dioxide since 1700? Circle your answer.

It has gone up. It has stayed the same. It has gone down.

b) Why has this happened? Tick the box next to your answer.

- We are burning lots of hydrogen gas. [ ]
- We are burning lots of fossil fuels. [ ]
- We have heated too much limestone. [ ]

Q3 The Earth is **warming up**.

a) What is this called?

....

b) Why is the Earth warming up? Tick the box next to the correct answer.

- [ ] Extra carbon dioxide is trapping heat.
- [ ] There is less carbon dioxide to cool the Earth down.

More Environmental Problems

Q4 Tick the boxes to show whether the following statements are **true** or **false**.

		True	False
a)	Oxygen is given out when trees are cut down.	☐	☐
b)	Living trees take in carbon dioxide for photosynthesis.	☐	☐
c)	Burning fossil fuels takes in carbon dioxide from the atmosphere.	☐	☐

Q5 Humans can affect the carbon dioxide level by **deforestation**.

a) What is deforestation? Circle your answer.

cutting down trees **planting new trees**

b) Circle the words to complete these sentences.

Living trees **increase** / **reduce** the amount of carbon dioxide in the atmosphere.

Deforestation means there is **more** / **less** carbon dioxide left in the atmosphere.

Q6 Which one of these is a way of **removing** carbon dioxide from the atmosphere? Tick the correct answer.

Releasing sulfur dioxide into the atmosphere. ☐

Burning hydrocarbons. ☐

Converting carbon dioxide into hydrocarbons. ☐

Q7 **Iron** can be used to **remove** carbon dioxide from the atmosphere.

Circle the word to complete these sentences.

Iron can be added to the **atmosphere** / **oceans**.

This is called iron **seeding** / **extraction**.

The iron helps more **plants** / **clouds** to grow.

These remove carbon dioxide from the atmosphere during **photosynthesis** / **deforestation**.

Biofuels

Q1 Biofuels can be used instead of fossil fuels.

a) What are biofuels made from? Circle your answer.

sea creatures   iron   crude oil   plants

b) Which of these is an advantage of using biofuels? Tick one box.

They make cars go faster.	☐
We don't use as much petrol.	☐
Cars that use biofuels won't break down.	☐

Q2 Circle the word to complete these sentences.

One example of a biofuel is **diesel / ethanol**.

It is made from **sugar cane / cotton** plants.

This means there is **more / less** space for growing food.

There are advantages though. Biofuels **will / won't** run out.

Q3 Wendy and George are talking about biofuels. One of them is **wrong**.

Biofuels don't make any carbon dioxide when they burn.

Biofuels do make carbon dioxide when they burn. But this is balanced out by the carbon dioxide taken in as the plants grew.

WENDY

GEORGE

Who is **right**, Wendy or George?

....

Fuel Cells

Q1 A **hydrogen-oxygen fuel cell** can be used to make electricity.

a) What is given off from a hydrogen-oxygen fuel cell? Tick the answer.

just carbon dioxide ☐ just water ☐ carbon dioxide and water ☐

b) Give **one** place where hydrogen-oxygen fuel cells are used. Circle your answer.

power station cars home heating camping stove

Q2 **Hydrogen gas** can be used as a fuel rather than petrol.

a) Which of these are advantages of using hydrogen-oxygen fuel cells? Tick **two** boxes.

Hydrogen is not a fossil fuel. ☐ The fuel cells make petrol. ☐

Less energy is wasted as heat. ☐

b) Give **one other advantage** of using hydrogen-oxygen fuel cells.

....

Q3 Give **three disadvantages** of using hydrogen gas as a fuel.

DISADVANTAGES OF USING HYDROGEN GAS AS A FUEL

1. ....

2. ....

3. ....

Barry 4 Karen

Think about where hydrogen comes from, how it's stored and if there are any dangers.

Measuring the Energy Content of Fuels

Q1 What is the **energy content** of a fuel? Circle your answer.

The amount of energy taken in when a fuel is burnt.

The amount of energy given out when a fuel is burnt.

Q2 Izzy is measuring the **energy content** of two fuels.

a) The diagram below shows the equipment Izzy uses. Fill in the labels on the diagram.

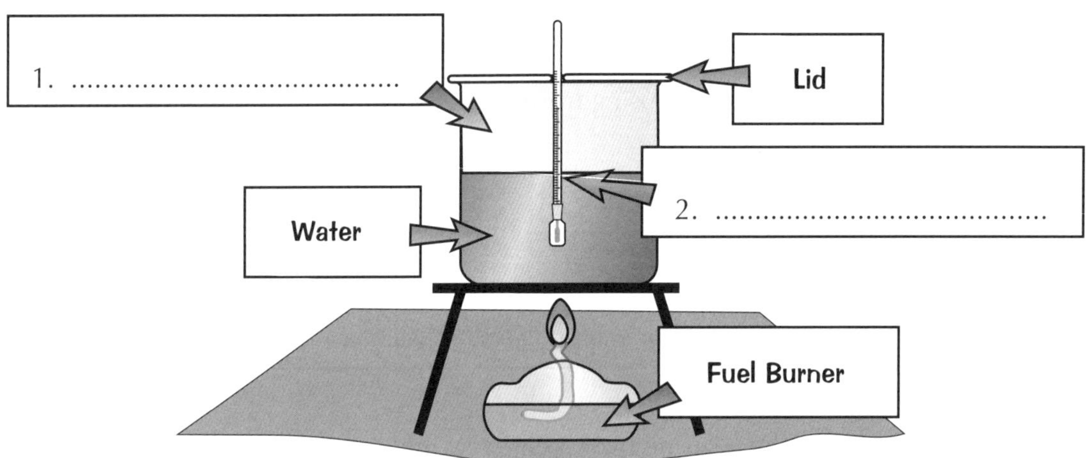

b) Circle the correct words in the sentence below.

Izzy needs to use **the same amount / different amounts** of water for each fuel.

c) Izzy's results are in the table below. They show how much of the two fuels (A and B) was needed to heat the water by 25 °C.

Fuel	Amount of fuel burnt (g)
A	6
B	13

Which fuel had the highest energy content? Circle your answer.

Fuel A **Fuel B**

Alkanes and Alkenes

Q1 Are these sentences true or false? Tick the boxes.

	True	False
a) Alkenes have only single bonds between the carbon atoms.	☐	☐
b) Alkenes are unsaturated.	☐	☐
c) Alkanes have only single bonds between the carbon atoms.	☐	☐

Q2 a) Below are the **first three alkanes**. Draw lines to match the structures to their names.

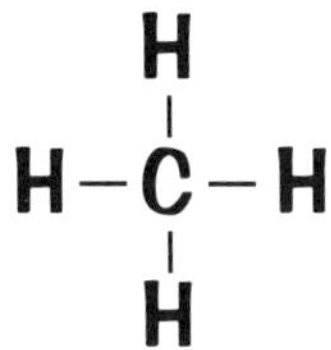

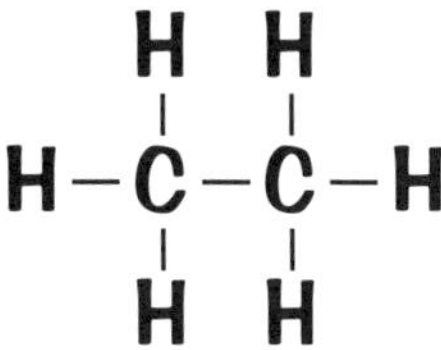

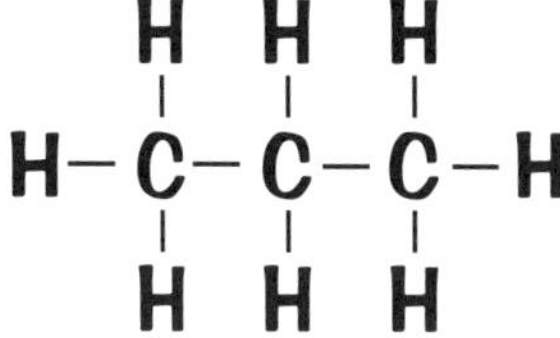

Ethane **Propane** **Methane**

b) Circle the right word in the sentence below.

Alkanes are **saturated / unsaturated** hydrocarbons.

Q3 Complete this table with the names of the alkenes.

Name of alkene	Formula
a)	$H_2C=CH_2$
b)	$H_2C=CH-CH_3$

Q4 Circle the right word in the sentence.

An alkene will turn bromine water from orangey brown to **yellow / colourless**.

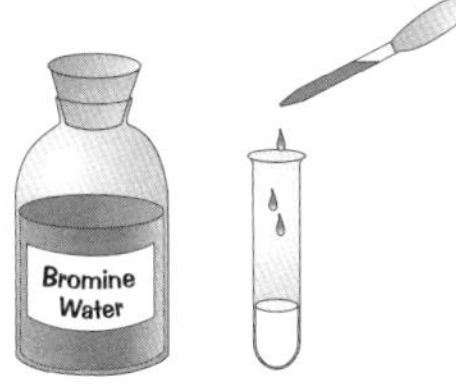

Cracking Hydrocarbons

Q1 Circle the right words in the sentences.

Long hydrocarbons can be turned into **shorter** / **longer** ones.

This is called **filtering** / **cracking**.

The shorter hydrocarbons are called alkanes and **polymers** / **alkenes**.

These are **more** / **less** useful than long hydrocarbons.

The shorter hydrocarbons can be used as **biofuels** / **fuels**.

Q2 The equipment shown below can be used to crack **paraffin**.

a) Label the diagram to show how paraffin can be cracked.
Write A, B and C in the boxes.

A Heat the paraffin and porcelain chips using a Bunsen burner

B Gas collects in the gas jar.

C The paraffin passes over the porcelain and is cracked.

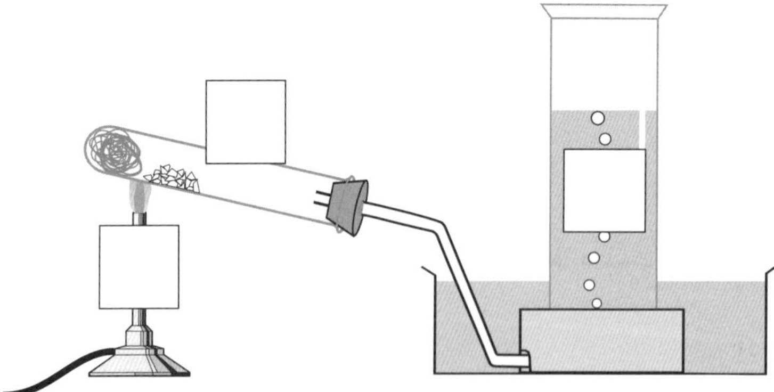

b) What gas collects in the gas jar? Circle your answer.

water vapour　　　small alkanes and alkenes　　　carbon dioxide

c) What could you use to test for **alkenes** at the end of the experiment?

....

Using Alkenes to Make Polymers

Q1 The diagram below shows a **polymer** being made.

$$3\ \mathrm{CH_2{=}CH_2} \rightarrow -\mathrm{CH_2{-}CH_2{-}CH_2{-}CH_2{-}CH_2{-}CH_2}-$$

a) What is the monomer in this reaction? Circle your answer.

$-\mathrm{CH_2{-}CH_2{-}CH_2{-}CH_2{-}CH_2{-}CH_2}-$ $\mathrm{CH_2{=}CH_2}$ $\mathrm{H{-}CH_2{-}CH_2{-}H}$

b) What is the name of the polymer made in this reaction? Circle your answer.

Poly(methane)   Poly(propene)   Poly(ethene)

c) What name is given to this process? Circle your answer.

fractional distillation   cracking   polymerisation

Q2 The table shows the **properties** of **two** polymers.

Polymer	Properties
PTFE	doesn't catch fire easily, tough
Poly(ethene)	stretchy, light

a) Which polymer should be used for **plastic bags**?

....

b) Which polymer should be used for coating **frying pans**?

....

Q3 Polymers can be **biodegradable** or **non-biodegradable**.

a) Draw lines to match the term with what it means.

Biodegradable polymers   They rot in the soil or break down in sunlight.

Non-biodegradable polymers   They won't rot.

b) What is the problem with **burning** polymers to get rid of them?

....

Mixed Questions — C1b Topics 3, 4 & 5

Q1 a) Tick the sentences that are **true**.

- ☐ Most metals are found as ores in the ground.
- ☐ All metals are extracted by electrolysis.
- ☐ No metals corrode.
- ☐ A metal can be made more useful by turning it into an alloy.
- ☐ It costs nothing to recycle metals.

b) Circle the right word in the sentence.

Steel alloys are **harder** / **softer** than pure iron.

Q2 Draw lines to match the products to the processes used to make them.

Aluminium	Electrolysis of sea water
Iron	Electrolysis of aluminium oxide
Chlorine	Reduction with carbon

Q3 Look at the information in the table below.

R, S, T and U are all metals.

Metal	Strength	Weight
R	Strong	Light
S	Quite Strong	Quite Light
T	Strong	Quite Heavy
U	Weak	Heavy

a) Which metal would be the best for building an **aeroplane**? ....

b) Give two reasons for your answer.

1. ....

2. ....

Mixed Questions — C1b Topics 3, 4 & 5

Q4 What is the process of **splitting up** long hydrocarbons called? Circle your answer.

polymerisation electrolysis cracking

Q5 The diagram below shows a polymer called poly(ethene).
Draw and name the **monomer** used to make this polymer.

POLYMER

```
  H H H H H H
  | | | | | |
—C-C-C-C-C-C—
  | | | | | |
  H H H H H H
```

MONOMER

Name:

Q6 Diesel is made of **long hydrocarbons**. Petrol is made of **short hydrocarbons**.

a) Complete the list below to show the **properties** of petrol and diesel.

Don't think of them as petrol and diesel. Think of them as short and long hydrocarbons.

DIESEL	PETROL
Viscous	1. ....
High boiling point	2. ....
Hard to set on fire	3. ....

b) There are three different fuels in the table. Fill in the table by writing '**yes**' or '**no**'.

Two have been done for you.

Fuel	Does using it in a car make carbon dioxide?	Will it run out?
Hydrogen gas (in a hydrogen-oxygen fuel cell)		No
Ethanol	Yes	
Petrol		

Changing Ideas About the Solar System

Q1 Complete the sentences. Use the words below them.

a) The **geocentric** model says the Sun and planets all orbit the ....

Solar System Moon Earth

b) The **heliocentric** model says that all the planets orbit the ....

Sun Moon Earth

c) In the **heliocentric** model the planets orbits are ....

circles ellipses spirals

d) Now we think that the .... of the orbits is different to the heliocentric model.

centre shape speed

Q2 **Galileo** was a scientist in the 1600s.

a) What did Galileo use to find proof for the heliocentric model? Circle the answer.

compass telescope seismometer

b) Galileo saw moons orbiting Jupiter.
What did this show about the Solar System? Tick the box.

- ☐ It showed that not everything orbits the Earth.
- ☐ It showed that the Sun orbits Jupiter.
- ☐ It showed that Jupiter was the centre of the Universe.
- ☐ It showed that Jupiter orbits Saturn.

c) Tick the box next to the **true** sentence below.

☐ You can see all the planets just using your eyes.

☐ Some planets were only discovered after the telescope was invented.

☐ Before the telescope was invented we knew about all of the planets.

Waves and the Universe

Q1 Are these sentences **true** or **false**? Tick the boxes.

		True	False
a)	Invisible light is the light that you can see.	☐	☐
b)	Light is a type of wave.	☐	☐
c)	Scientists can use visible light to learn about the Universe.	☐	☐
d)	We live in the Milky Way galaxy.	☐	☐
e)	We can see galaxies because they give out infrared radiation.	☐	☐
f)	We can see moons and planets because they give out light.	☐	☐

Q2 Draw lines to match up each way of looking at the Universe with its description.

Telescopes

Looking with the naked eye

Photographs

Can only be used to see things that are really big and bright, or really near Earth.

Can be used to magnify the things you're looking at.

Can be used to record what something looks like.

Q3 Label the pictures below with what was used to look at them. Use words from the box.

Looking with the naked eye	Telescope	Photograph

a) .... b) .... c) ....

Q4 Give **two good points** about using **photography** to look at the Universe.

1. ....

2. ....

Waves — The Basics (1)

Q1 Circle the right word in the sentence below.

Waves transfer **energy / matter** and information from one place to another.

Q2 Draw lines to match the words with their descriptions.

Wavelength	How many waves pass a certain point every second.
Frequency	The distance from the rest position to a crest or a trough.
Amplitude	The length of a full cycle of a wave.

Q3 Diagrams **A**, **B** and **C** are pictures of waves.

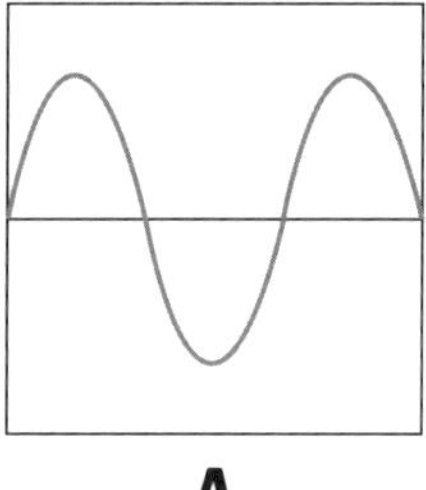
A

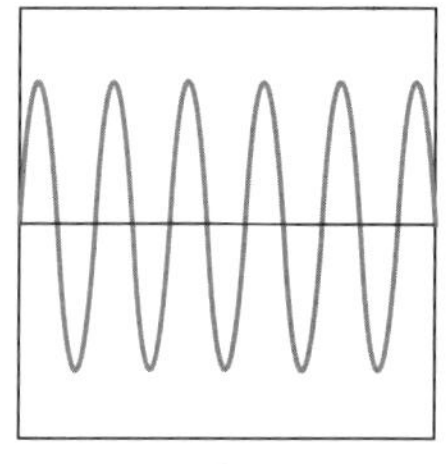
B

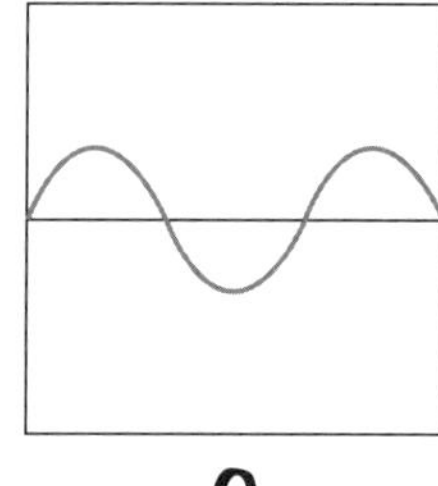
C

a) Which two diagrams show waves with the same **frequency**? .... and ....

b) Which two diagrams show waves with the same **amplitude**? .... and ....

c) Which two diagrams show waves with the same **wavelength**? .... and ....

Q4 A wave travels **12 m** in **5 seconds**. Complete the calculation to find the speed of the wave.

wave speed = distance / time

wave speed = ... / ....

wave speed = ... m/s

Waves — The Basics (2)

Q1 Draw lines to match each wave with its **name**.

Transverse

Longitudinal

Q2 Circle the waves that are **transverse**.

sound | P-waves | electromagnetic (EM) | S-waves

Example: A wave has a wavelength of **2 m** and a frequency of **125 Hz**. Calculate the **speed** of the wave.

Write out the formula for wave speed that includes wavelength and frequency.

wave speed = frequency × wavelength

wave speed = 125 Hz × 2 m = 250 m/s

Don't forget to write the correct units.

Plug the numbers in.

Work out the answer with a calculator.

Q3 A **sound wave** has a wavelength of **4 m** and a frequency of **85 Hz**.

Calculate the **speed** of the sound wave.

wave speed = frequency × wavelength

....

.... m/s

Q4 A **water wave** has a frequency of **2.5 Hz** and a wavelength of **1.2 m**.

Tick the box next to the **speed** of the water wave.

3 m/s ☐ 0.48 m/s ☐

3.7 m/s ☐ 2.08 Hz ☐

Reflection, Refraction and Lenses

Q1 Complete the sentences. Use words from the box.

reflection	boundary	refraction

a) A .... is a place where two materials meet.

b) When a wave hits a boundary it can bounce back.

This is called ....

c) A wave can change direction when it crosses a boundary.

This is called ....

Q2 Tick the boxes to show if the waves have been **reflected** or **refracted**.

a)

Material 2

Material 1

Wave

Reflected ☐

Refracted ☐

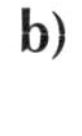

b)

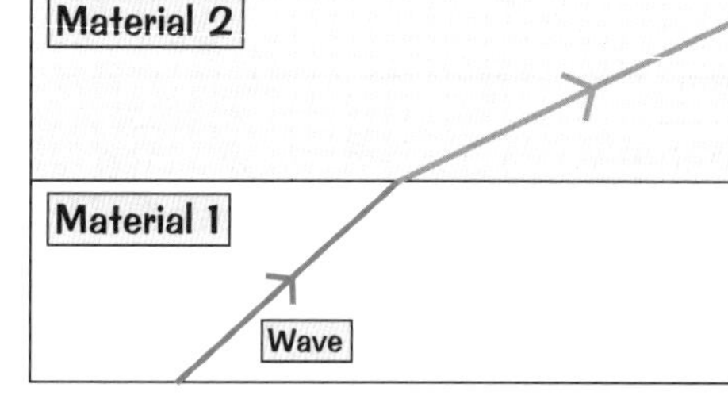

Reflected ☐

Refracted ☐

Q3 Label the diagram of light passing through a lens. Use words from the box.

focal point	axis	focal length

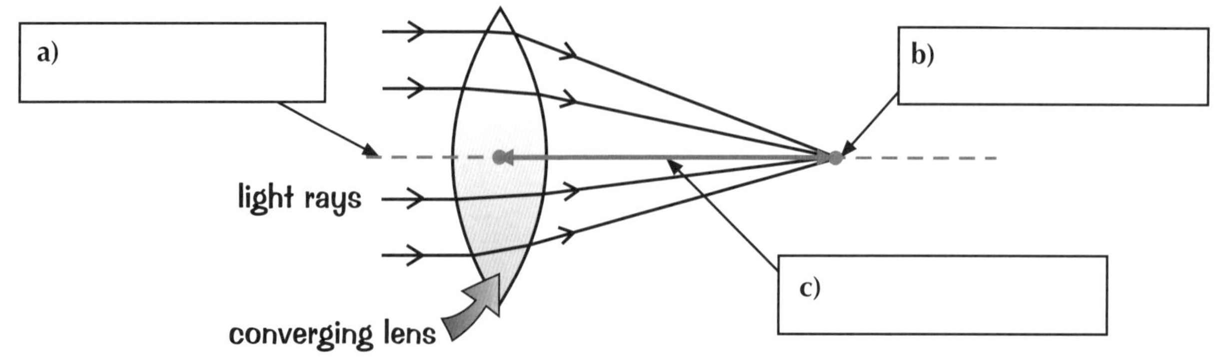

Ray Diagrams

Q1 **Ray diagrams** show how light from an object passes through a lens to form a image.

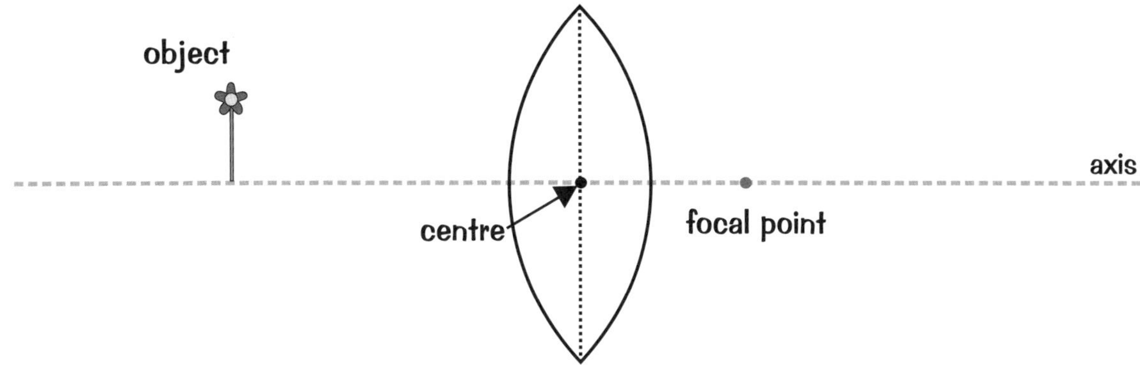

a) On the diagram, draw a ray from the top of the object straight through the centre of the lens.

b) Draw a ray going from the top of the object in the same direction as the axis.
This ray should stop in the middle of the lens.

c) Draw a ray from the end of the ray drawn in part **b)** through the focal point.

d) Draw in the image of the object.

Q2 Draw the **light rays** and the **image** to complete the ray diagram.

You can use the steps from **Q1** to help you.

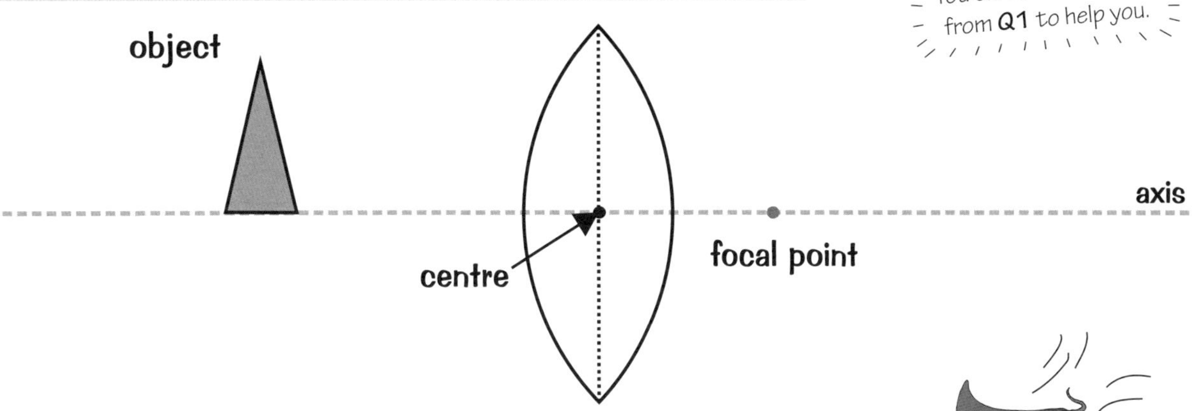

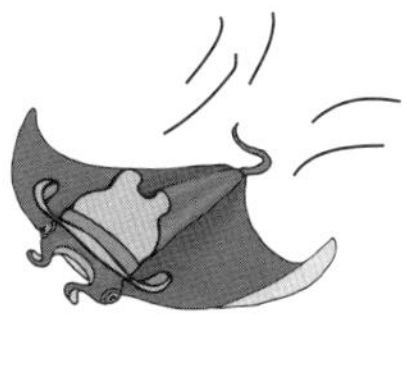

Q3 Draw the **light rays** and the **image** to complete the ray diagram.

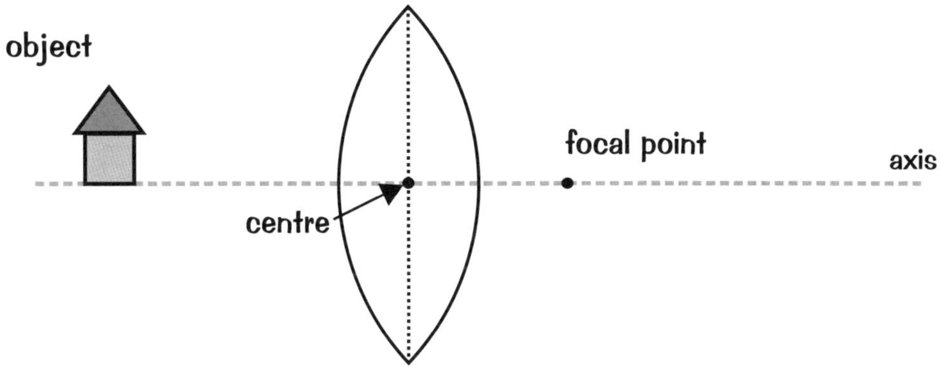

Lenses and Images

Q1 The diagram shows an image being formed on a **screen**.

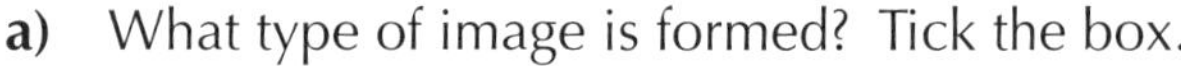

a) What type of image is formed? Tick the box.

Real ☐

Virtual ☐

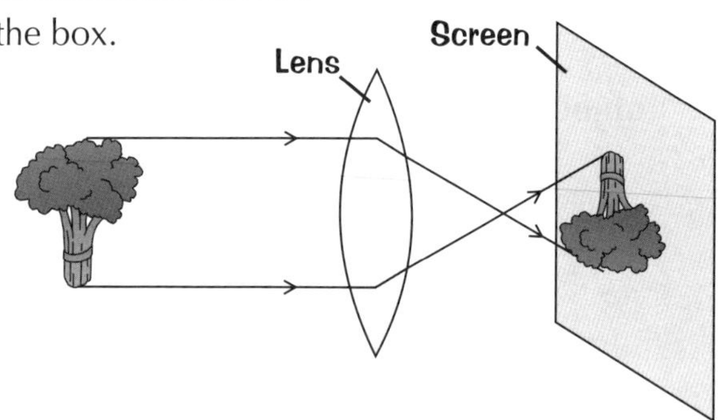

b) What happens to the light as it goes through the lens? Circle the answer.

It is reflected. | It is diffracted. | It is refracted.

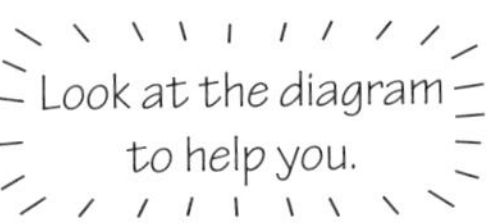

Q2 The **equipment** shown below can be used to measure the **focal length** of a lens.

a) Complete the labels on the diagram. Use words from the box.

ruler	clamp	white card	track	converging lens

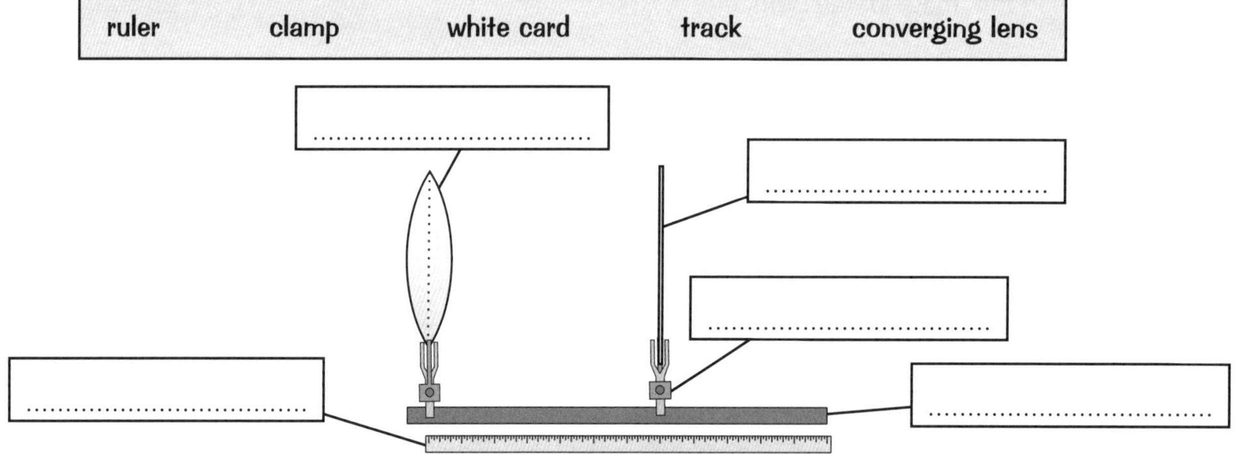

b) How can you tell when the lens and the card are a **focal length apart**? Circle the answer.

The image is blurry. | It's always 10 cm. | The image is the sharpest you can get it.

Q3 Draw lines to match the sentences to the type of image they describe.

The image can be formed on a screen. — Virtual

The image appears to come from a different place than the object. — Real

Telescopes

Q1 The diagram shows someone using a **simple telescope** to look at a planet.

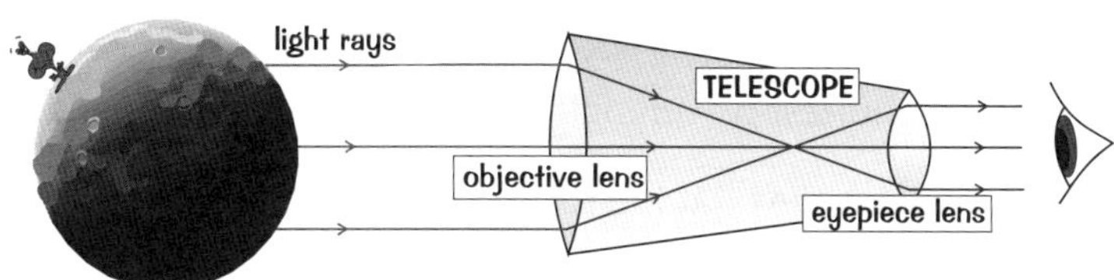

a) Which lens **focuses** light and forms a **real image**? Circle the answer.

objective lens **eyepiece lens**

b) Which lens **magnifies** the image? Circle the answer.

objective lens **eyepiece lens**

Q2 **Reflecting telescopes** are made from curved mirrors.

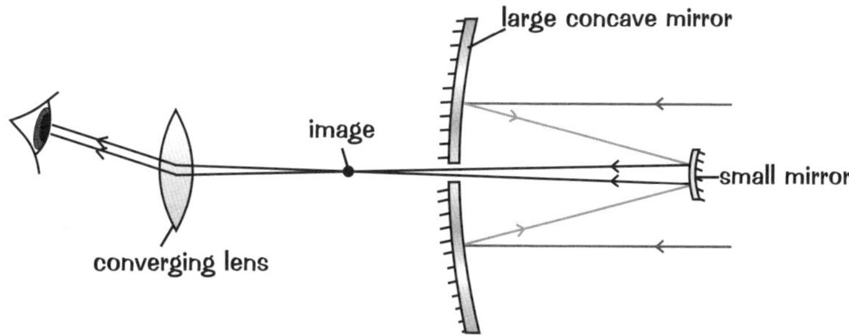

a) Tick the box to show what **type** of image is formed.

Real ☐ **Virtual** ☐

b) What is the **large concave mirror** used for? Tick **two** boxes.

It is used to magnify the image. ☐

It is used to collect light from an object. ☐

It reflects light onto the smaller mirror. ☐

It is used to refract light onto the small mirror. ☐

c) Complete the sentences below. Use words from the box.

reflects **behind** **hole** **magnifies**

The small mirror .... the light from the large mirror.

The light passes through a .... in the centre of the large mirror.

A real image is formed .... the mirror where the rays cross.

A converging lens .... the image.

Electromagnetic Waves

Q1 Are these sentences **true** or **false**? Tick the boxes.

		True	False
a)	All electromagnetic waves are transverse waves.	☐	☐
b)	Radio waves have the shortest wavelength of all electromagnetic waves.	☐	☐
c)	All electromagnetic waves travel at the same speed in a vacuum.	☐	☐

Q2 Complete the labels on the electromagnetic spectrum. Use words from the list.

Infrared X-rays Microwaves Ultraviolet

Radio Waves			Visible Light			Gamma Rays

Lowest Frequency → Highest Frequency

Q3 Circle the right words in the sentences below.

Herschel discovered **ultraviolet / infrared** radiation.

He split up light with a **prism / lens**.

He then measured the **temperature / wavelength** of the different colours of light.

He found that the **coldest / hottest** bit was invisible and just past the red light.

Q4 Which of these things are the same for microwaves and X-rays? Tick the boxes.

- ☐ frequency
- ☐ they are both transverse waves
- ☐ speed in a vacuum
- ☐ wavelength

Mr. Microwave

Mrs. X-ray

Electromagnetic Waves

Q5 Ritter discovered a type of **invisible radiation**. His experiment is shown below.

Complete the labels on the diagram. Use words from the box.
One has been done for you.

~~silver chloride on paper strips~~	prism	stopwatch	white light

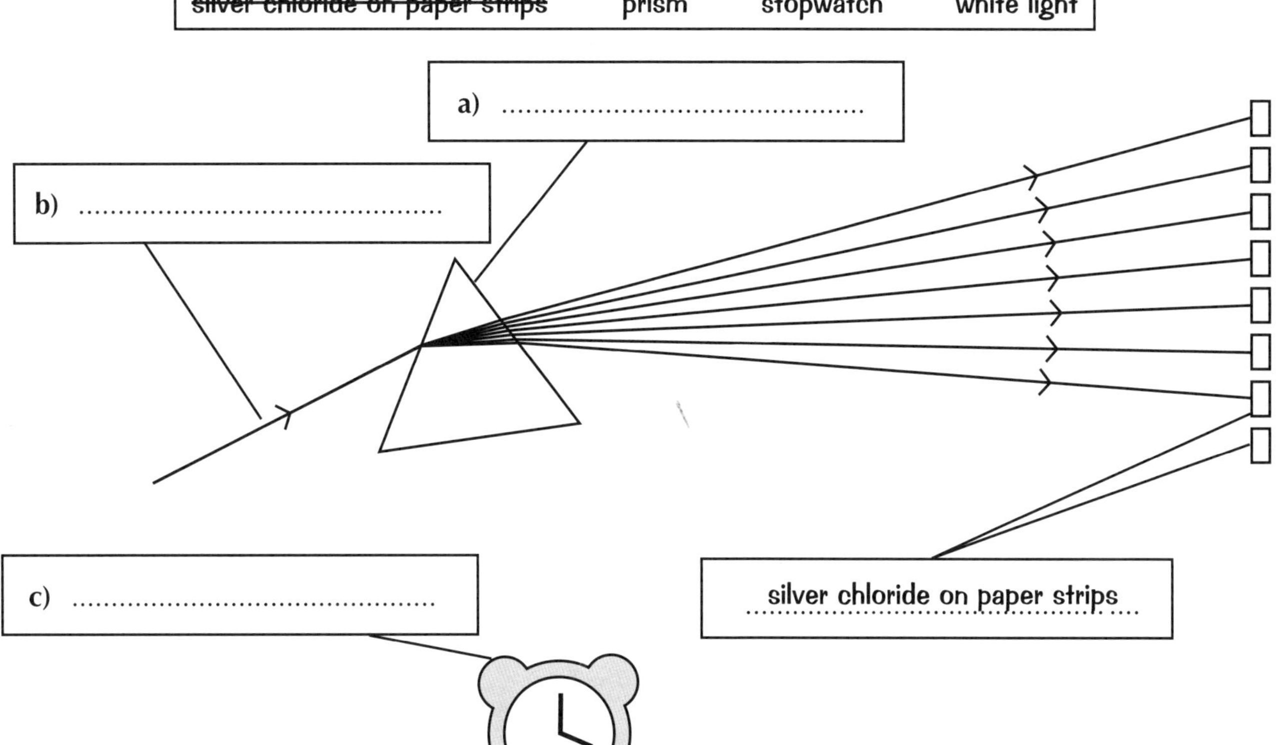

Q6 When silver chloride is exposed to **light**, it turns from **white** to **black**.

a) What did Ritter find when he exposed silver chloride strips to **each colour** of light?
Tick the box.

☐ The strips turned to black **quickest** near the **violet** end of the spectrum.

☐ **All** the strips took exactly the **same amount** of time to turn from white to black.

☐ The strips turned to black **quickest** near the **red** end of the spectrum.

b) Which type of radiation did Ritter discover? Circle the answer.

The Dangers of Electromagnetic Radiation

Q1 Complete the sentences using the words in the boxes.

Visible light waves **Gamma rays** **Microwaves**

a) .... have a **lower frequency** than infrared.

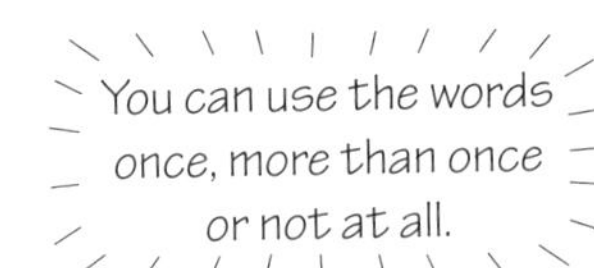

b) .... have a **higher frequency** than X-rays.

c) .... are the **most dangerous** type of wave.

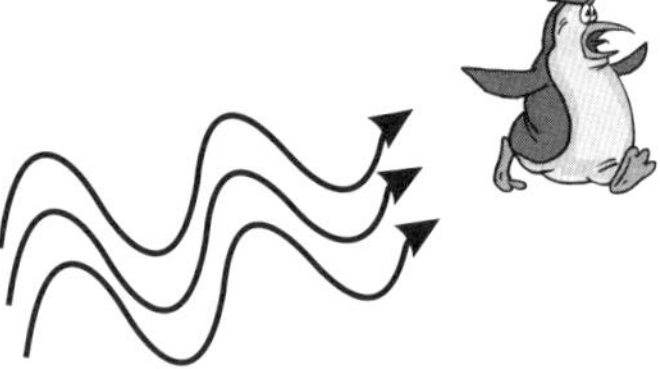

Q2 Circle the right words in the sentences below.

a) The danger from EM waves **increases / decreases** as their frequency increases.

b) High-frequency EM waves are the **most / least** dangerous.

c) Low-frequency EM waves are **more dangerous / safer**.

Q3 Different types of EM radiation can cause different **problems**. Put **all** the problems from the box into the table below.

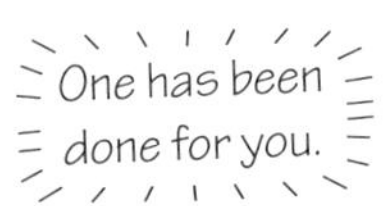

sunburn heating body cells skin burns
cell mutation ~~cancer~~ skin cancer

Type of EM Radiation	Problems it can cause
Microwaves	
Infrared	
Ultraviolet	
Gamma / X-rays	cancer

Radio Waves and Microwaves

Q1 Circle **three** uses of **radio waves** below.

transmitting satellite signals

burglar alarms

sterilising medical equipment

broadcasting TV signals

communicating

heating food

Q2 Microwaves are used in microwave ovens to **cook** food.

a) What substance in food **absorbs energy** from microwaves? Circle the answer.

carbon salt protein water

Extra Large Popcorn

b) What happens to substances when they absorb microwave energy? Tick one box.

- [ ] They heat up.
- [ ] They get charged.
- [ ] They give out light.

Q3 Microwaves are used to send **satellite TV signals**.

a) Complete the labels on the diagram to show how this works.
Use words from the box.

Satellite picks up signal

C

B

A

Signal picked up by dish

Satellite sends signal to Earth

Microwaves

Transmitter sends out signal

b) What other type of communication uses microwaves?
Tick the box.

- [ ] mobile phones
- [ ] radio signals
- [ ] landline phones

Infrared Radiation

Q1 Complete the sentences using words from the box.

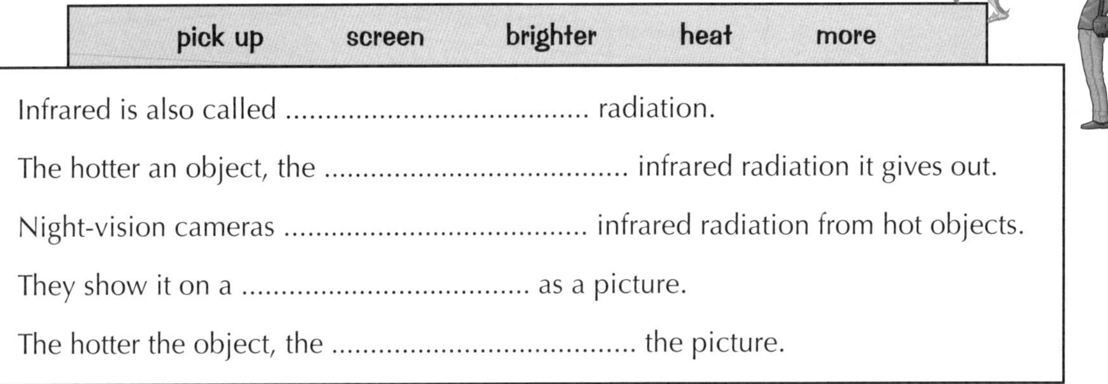

pick up **screen** **brighter** **heat** **more**

Infrared is also called .... radiation.

The hotter an object, the .... infrared radiation it gives out.

Night-vision cameras .... infrared radiation from hot objects.

They show it on a .... as a picture.

The hotter the object, the .... the picture.

Q2 Information can be sent through **optical fibres**.

a) Tick the boxes next to the sentences that are **true**.

☐ Optical fibres carry information over long distances.

☐ Optical fibres carry sound waves.

☐ Optical fibres are used in telephone cables.

b) Which type of radiation is used in optical fibres?
Circle **one** answer.

Ultraviolet **Microwaves** **Infrared** **Radio**

Q3 Infrared radiation can be used to **send information** between mobile phones and computers.

a) Circle the right word in the sentence.

Infrared radiation can be sent over **short / long** distances between mobile phones and computers.

b) Name **two** other ways that infrared radiation can be used in the home.

1. ....

2. ....

Visible Light, UV and X-rays

Q1 Complete the sentences about **visible light**.
Use words from the boxes under each sentence.

a) We can see some objects because they are ....

illuminated	invisible	infrared

b) We can see other objects because they .... light.

absorb	reflect

c) For us to see an object, light from it needs to enter our ....

mouth	nose	eyes

Q2 a) What happens to fluorescent ink when it absorbs **ultraviolet radiation**? Tick the box.

It gives out visible light. ☐

It gives out ultraviolet radiation. ☐

It gives out X-rays. ☐

b) Circle the right words in the sentences below.

The ink in special security pens can only be seen in **infrared / ultraviolet** light.

The police can use the ink to identify your things if they are **melted / stolen**.

Banks use fluorescent ink when they make **bank notes / coins**.

Under UV lights, real ones show special markings, but fake ones just **glow / burn**.

Q3 Draw lines to join up the type of radiation with its **uses**.

X-rays

Ultraviolet radiation

Fluorescent lamps

Airport security scanners

To look inside objects

To look for broken bones

Disinfecting water

Gamma Rays and Ionising Radiation

Q1 Complete the sentences about **gamma rays**. Use words from the box.

carefully kill cancer normal

High doses of gamma radiation will .... living cells.

Because of this, gamma radiation is used to treat ....

The gamma rays are .... directed.

This is so they don't kill too many .... cells.

Q2 Number the steps below 1-4 to show how **gamma rays** can be used to **detect** cancer. One has been done for you.

☐ The camera makes a picture which can be used to look for cancer.

[1] A radioactive source is put into the patient's body.

☐ A special camera sees the gamma rays emitted from the source.

☐ The source travels around the body.

Q3 Which of these sentences are **true**? Tick the boxes.

Ionising radiation is given off all the time by radioactive sources. ☐

Ionising radiation from radioactive sources can be either beta, gamma or omega. ☐

All three types of ionising radiation transfer energy. ☐

Ionising radiation can knock protons off atoms. ☐

Q4 The diagram shows radiation being used to **sterilise** medical instruments.

radioactive source

a) What kind of electromagnetic radiation is used?

....

b) Name one other thing this radiation can be used to sterilise.

....

The Solar System

Q1 Which of the sentences below is **true**? Tick one box.

- ☐ Planets go round the Sun.
- ☐ The Sun is a galaxy.
- ☐ The Earth goes round the Moon.
- ☐ The Moon is the largest object in the Universe.

Q2 Complete the sentences on galaxies. Use words from the box.

stars Universe Milky Way

A galaxy is a collection of ....

Our Solar System is part of the .... galaxy.

All galaxies are in the ....

Q3 Fill in the gaps to put these things in **size** order.
Use words from the box.

galaxy star planet

moon → .... → .... → .... → Universe

Smallest ⟶ Largest

Q4 Number the distances 1-4 in order of **size**. The smallest should be 1 and the largest 4. One has been done for you.

	Distance between Earth and Sun
	Distance between stars
	Distance between galaxies
1	Distance between Earth and Moon

Is Anybody Out There?

Q1 Circle the right words in the sentences below.

> Landers are **robots** / **telescopes** that can be sent into space.
>
> They can be sent to a planet's surface to take **x-rays** / **photos** and samples.
>
> It's really **expensive** / **cheap** to send landers into space.

Q2 Scientists can gather information from space using **telescopes**, **probes** and **landers**.

a) Draw lines to match the type of equipment with its use. One has been done for you.

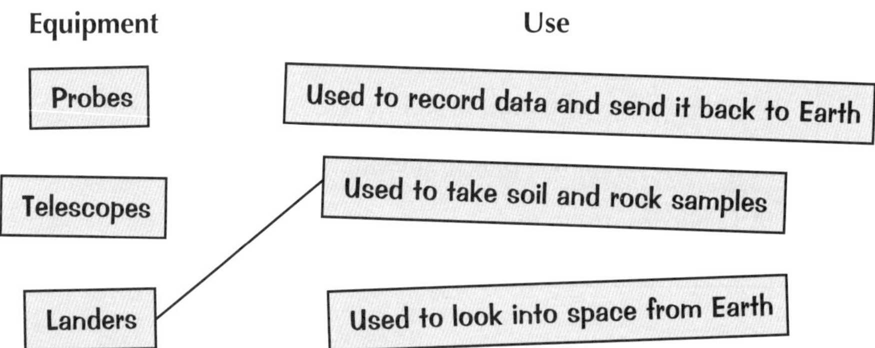

b) Why is it **better** to use telescopes instead of probes? Tick one box.

- [ ] We can get closer to planets and moons with telescopes.
- [ ] It's cheaper to use a telescope.
- [ ] We can use telescopes to take samples.

Q3 a) What does **SETI** stand for? Circle the letter next to the correct answer.

A — Seeking EarthTerrestrial Intelligence

B — Search for ExtraTerrestrial Intelligence

C — Society for ExtraTerrestrial Intelligence

D — Searching for ExtraTerrestrial Information

b) What do scientists on the SETI project listen for?

....

....

Looking into Space

Q1 Telescopes on **Earth** can have **problems** looking into space. What causes these problems? Tick **three** boxes.

- ☐ Air pollution
- ☐ Water pollution
- ☐ The Earth's atmosphere
- ☐ Light pollution

Q2 a) Complete the sentences. Use words from the box.

waves	space	telescopes

Stars give off .... from all parts of the electromagnetic spectrum.

Modern .... can detect these different waves.

This lets us 'see' things in .... that would normally be invisible.

b) What can we now 'see' because of modern telescopes? Circle **two** answers.

exploding stars microwave ovens aliens on Mars brown dwarfs

Q3 a) Circle the right words in the sentences below.

Magnification just means making something bigger.

Modern telescopes are **bigger** / **smaller** and better.

They have helped us to understand **less** / **more** about the Universe.

Bigger telescopes can pick up **less** / **more** light so we can see faint objects.

Better magnification lets us look further to find distant **galaxies** / **telescopes**.

b) Why is it good to link telescopes to computers? Tick one box.

- ☐ **Computers can look further into space than telescopes.**
- ☐ **Computers can collect samples from telescopes.**
- ☐ **We can store lots of data on computers to use later on.**

Space and Spectrometry

Q1 a) Complete the sentences. Use words from the list.

colours mix split microwaves

Spectrometers .... up light into a spectrum.

A spectrum is a band of .... like a rainbow.

b) Draw lines to match the **type of line** on a spectrum with what it shows.

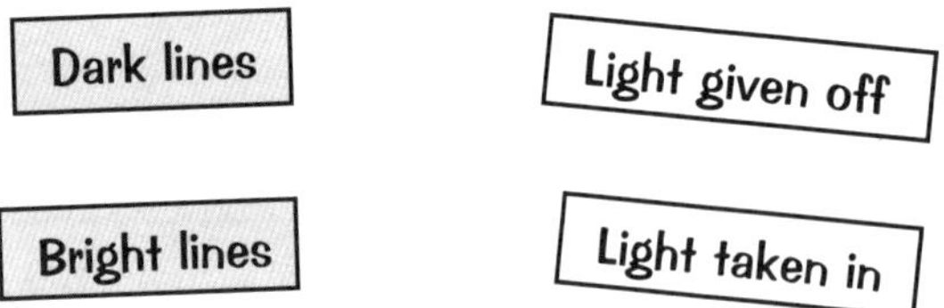

c) What can a spectrum tell us about galaxies and stars? Circle the answer.

What they smell like

If there's life on them

What they're made of

Q2 a) Add labels to this diagram of a simple spectrometer. Use words from the box.

slit for light source eyehole slit for CD

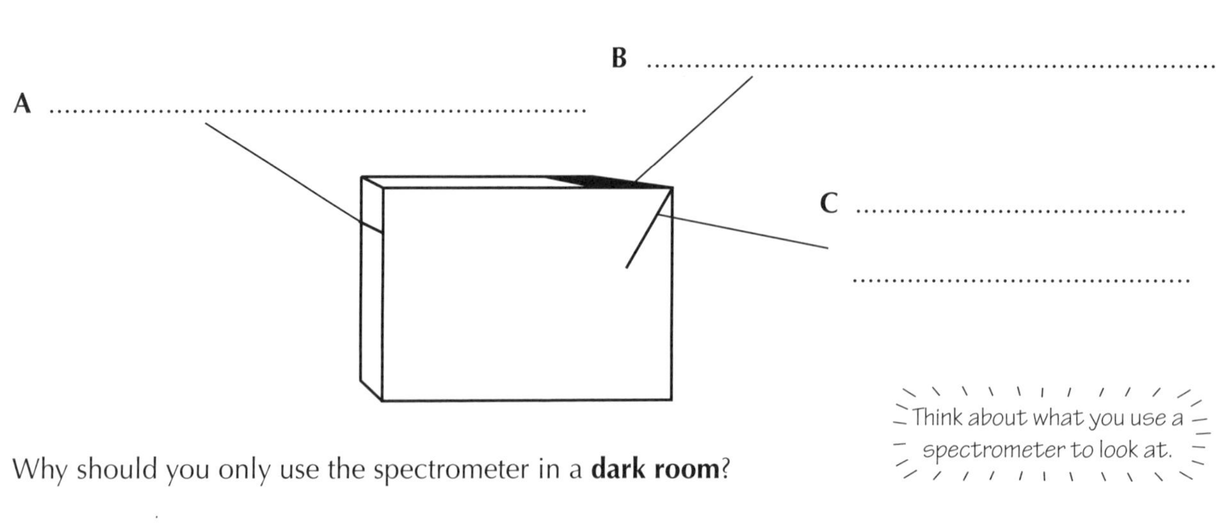

b) Why should you only use the spectrometer in a **dark room**?

....

The Life Cycle of Stars

Q1 Complete the labels on the diagram of the life cycle of a star. Use words from the box.

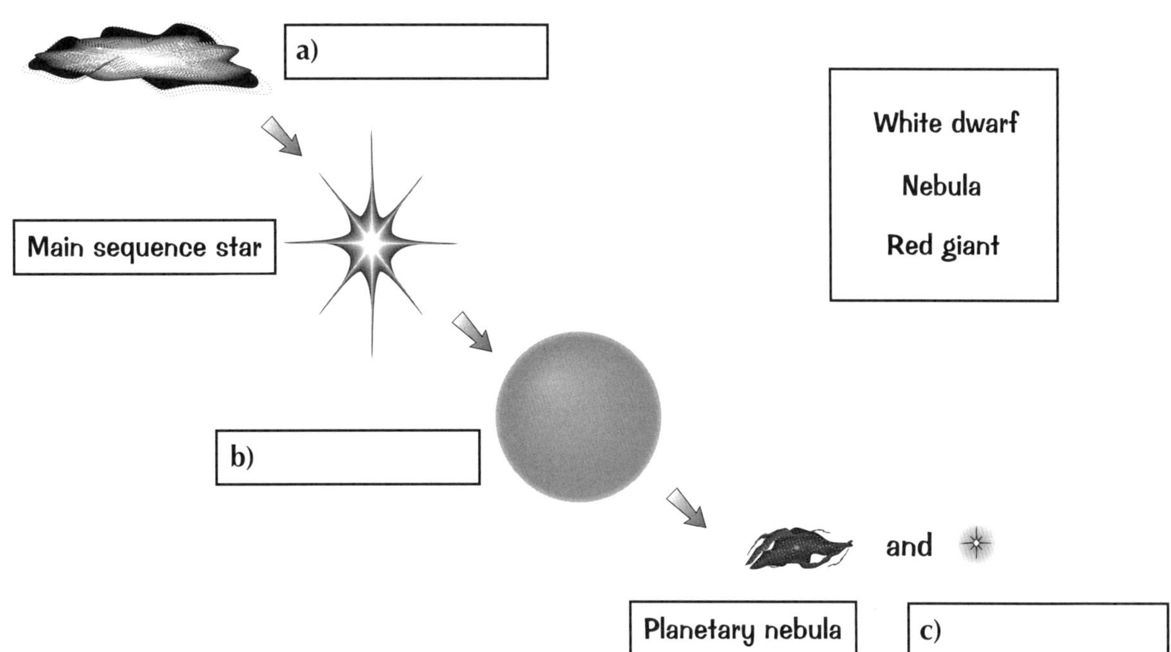

Q2 These sentences explain how a star is formed.

Write numbers 1-5 in the boxes to put the sentences in the **right order**.
One has been done for you.

- [ ] Fusion gives out lots of heat and light.
- [ ] A star is made.
- [ ] The heat makes fusion happen.
- [ ] Gravity pulls the dust and gas close together, making heat.
- [1] Clouds of dust and gas come together in a nebula.

Q3 Circle the right words in the sentences below.

A main sequence star will eventually run out of **hydrogen** / **gravity**. It then swells into a **nebula** / **red giant**. The star becomes **unstable** / **stable** and throws out gas and dust as a planetary nebula. This leaves a hot, small and heavy core called a **brown** / **white** dwarf.

The Origins of the Universe

Q1 There are two **theories** about where the Universe came from.

a) Draw lines to match each theory with its description.

Big Bang

Steady State

The Universe has always been here and will always be here.

Everything in the Universe was squashed into a tiny space. Then it exploded.

b) Tick the boxes next to **two** pieces of evidence for the Big Bang theory.

- ☐ Cosmic microwave background radiation
- ☐ A big hole in the Universe where the explosion happened
- ☐ Red-shift
- ☐ Satellite TV signals

c) Which theory do **most** people believe? Circle the answer.

Big Bang

Steady State

Q2 Circle the right words in the sentences below.

Light from distant galaxies seems to have a **shorter / longer** wavelength than it should.
This is called **red-shift / blue-shift**.
It tells us that most galaxies are moving **away from / towards** us very quickly.

Q3 **a)** What is **cosmic microwave background radiation**? Circle the answer.

Radiation coming from all parts of the Universe.

Radiation coming from old space shuttles.

Radiation coming from the backs of microwave ovens.

b) Where do scientists think cosmic microwave background radiation comes from?

....

Mixed Questions — P1a Topics 1, 2 & 3

Q1 All waves have a **frequency**.

a) What does frequency mean? Tick one box.

☐ How many whole waves pass a certain point each second.

☐ The length of a full cycle of a wave.

☐ The distance from the rest position to a trough of a wave.

b) A wave has a frequency of **5 Hz** and a wavelength of **2.5 m**.
Calculate the speed of the wave.

wave speed = frequency × wavelength

....

.... m/s

c) The diagram below shows the electromagnetic spectrum in order.
Which type of wave has the **highest frequency**? Circle the answer.

Radio Waves	Microwaves	Infrared	Visible Light	Ultraviolet	X-rays	Gamma Rays

d) Write down **one** use for each type of wave below.

Microwaves Use: ....

Visible light Use: ....

Q2 a) What type of electromagnetic wave does a **remote control** use?

....

b) Jake can change the TV channel by pointing the remote control at a mirror.
The diagram below shows the path of the wave from the remote control to the TV.
Complete the diagram by using words from the box.

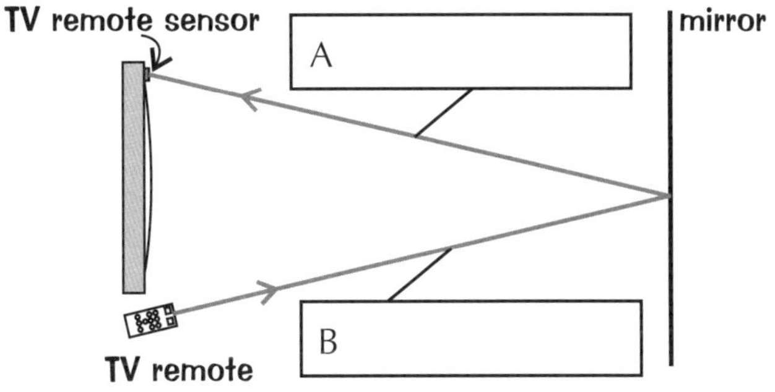

reflected ray

incoming ray

Mixed Questions — P1a Topics 1, 2 & 3

Q3 Lenses in telescopes **refract** light.

a) What does refract mean? Tick one box.

☐ The light changes direction as it enters the lens.

☐ The light bounces back as it enters the lens.

b) What **type** of lens do telescopes use? Circle the answer.

diverging **converging** **axis**

c) Are these sentences **true** or **false**? Tick the boxes.

	True	False
Telescopes are used to look into the oceans.	☐	☐
Some planets were only discovered after the telescope was invented.	☐	☐
Modern telescopes can only detect visible light.	☐	☐
Telescopes magnify images so we can see further.	☐	☐

Q4 a) Draw lines to match the model of the Solar System to its description.

Model	Description
Heliocentric	Earth at the centre. Everything orbits the Earth in circles.
Geocentric	Sun at the centre. Everything orbits the Sun in circles.

b) Which is larger, the Moon or the Sun? Circle the answer.

the Moon the Sun

c) Circle the right words in the sentences below.

You can see galaxies because they **give off / reflect** light.

You can see planets because they **give off / reflect** light.

Ultrasound

Q1 Circle the sentence about ultrasound that is **not true**.

A — Ultrasound waves are high frequency sound waves.

B — Ultrasound waves can't be reflected.

C — Ultrasound can be used to work out distances.

Q2 These sentences about ultrasound are **false**. Change each one so that it is true.

a) Ultrasound waves have frequencies below 20 000 Hz.

....

b) Ultrasound is a type of light wave.

....

Example: A pulse of ultrasound takes 2 seconds to travel to a wall and back again. The velocity of ultrasound in air is 300 m/s. How far away is the wall?

Write out the equation linking distance to velocity. → **distance = velocity × time**

distance = 300 m/s × 2 s = 600 m ← Plug the numbers in.

distance to the wall = 600 m ÷ 2 = 300 m ← Don't forget to write the correct units.

The distance to the wall is only half the total distance, so divide by two.

Q3 A pulse of ultrasound takes **1 second** to go from a boat to the seabed and back again.

a) The velocity of sound in the water is **1500 m/s**.
Complete the calculation below to find the total distance the wave travels.

Distance = velocity × time

Distance = ... × .... = ... m

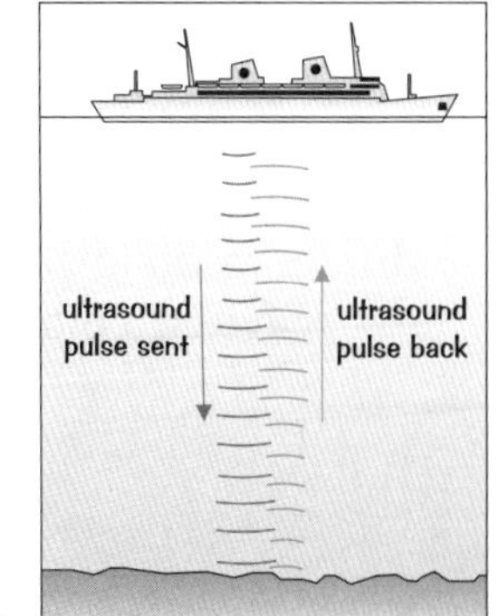

b) How far away is the seabed?

....

.... m

Ultrasound and Infrasound

Q1 The picture shows a submarine using **ultrasound** to find a whale.

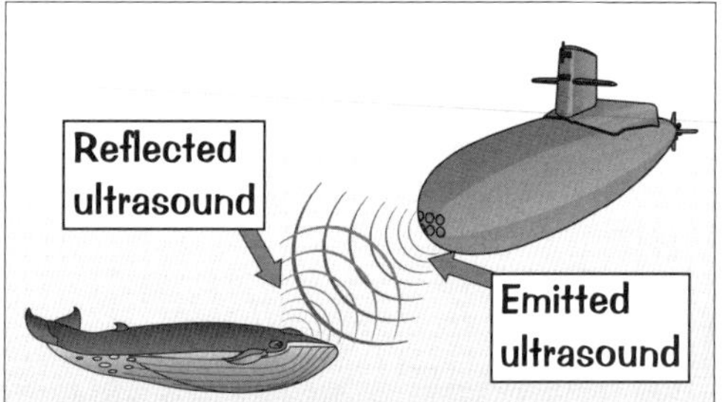

a) What is the name of this use of ultrasound? Circle the answer below.

Radar

Sonar

Infrasound

b) How do **animals** use ultrasound? Tick the box.

☐ For communicating

☐ For eating

Q2 Complete the sentences using words from the box.

growing reflections body

Ultrasound waves can pass through the .... to an unborn baby inside.

A computer makes a picture from ultrasound ....

This helps the doctor to check that the baby is ....

Q3 Some animals use **infrasound** to communicate.

a) Circle the right words in the sentences about infrasound.

Sound with frequencies of less than **20 / 20 000** Hz is known as infrasound.

Infrasound is used by animals to communicate over **short / long** distances.

b) Infrasound can be used to track animals in remote places.
Give **two other** things that infrasound could be used to detect.

1. ....

2. ....

The Earth's Structure

Q1 Circle the right words in these sentences about the Earth.

The Earth has a **crust / shell**, mantle and a core.

The core is at the **edge / centre** of the Earth.

The Earth's top layer is made up of **large / small** pieces called tectonic plates.

Convection currents in the mantle make the plates **move / stay still**.

Q2 Are these sentences **true** or **false**? Tick the boxes.

a) The mantle inside the Earth flows like a liquid.

b) The crust is broken into bits.

c) Tectonic plates can't move.

d) Tectonic plates can slide past each other.

e) Earthquakes are caused by the pull of the Moon.

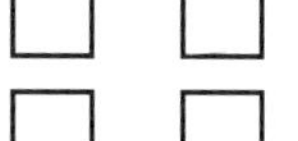

f) Earthquakes are caused by the movement of tectonic plates.

Q3 Lara does the experiment below to find out about earthquakes.

a) The brick and the sandpaper act like parts of the Earth. Which parts? Tick the box.

☐ The crust and the core.

☐ The tectonic plates.

☐ The sea and the crust.

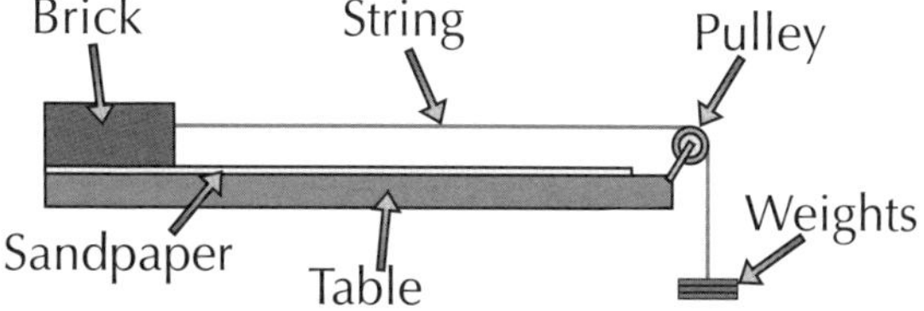

b) What will happen to the brick when Lara adds enough weight to the string?

....

c) Lara does the experiment three times. She gets different results each time. What does this show about real earthquakes? Circle the answer.

You can't predict them. **They cause a lot of damage.**

Seismic Waves

Q1 Draw lines to match each word with its description. One has been done for you.

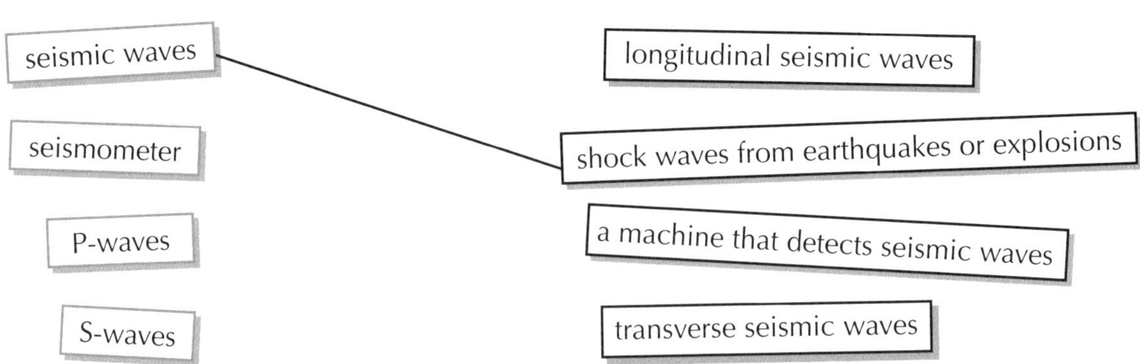

Q2 Waves can **change direction** or **bounce back** as they travel through materials. Complete the labels on the diagrams below. Use the words in the box.

Words can be used more than once.

Boundary	Reflection	Refraction

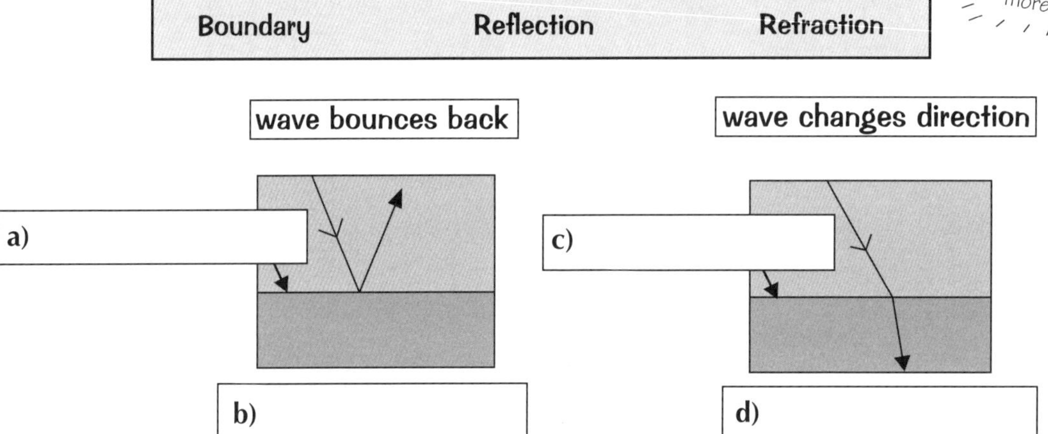

Q3 The diagram shows how you can work out where an earthquake happened.

Complete the sentences to explain the diagram. Use words from the box.

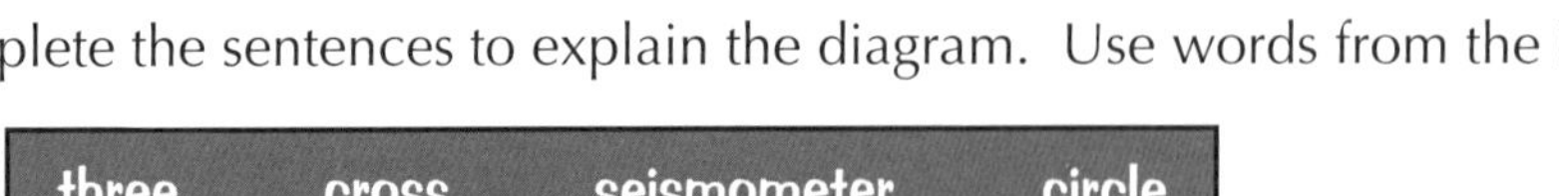

You can use a .... to calculate the distance to an earthquake. Using this distance, you can draw a .... on a map with the seismometer at the centre. You need .... seismometers to find the location of an earthquake. The earthquake happened at the point where the circles ....

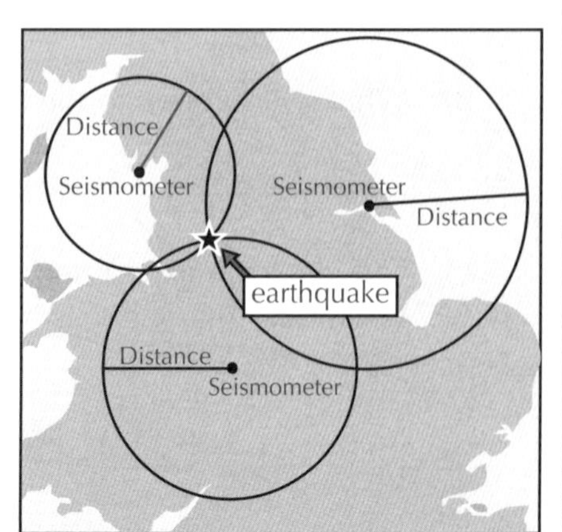

Electric Current and Power

Q1 Draw lines to match the sentences below to **voltage** or **current**.
One has been done for you.

- An electrical pressure that pushes charge around a circuit. — voltage
- This is measured in amps.
- This is a measure of how much energy is transferred.
- This is measured in volts.
- This is the rate of flow of charge around a circuit.

voltage

current

Q2 a) Which of these sentences describes **alternating current** (a.c.)? Circle the answer.

It keeps changing its direction.

It always flows in the same direction.

b) Name the other type of current.

....

Q3 Circle the right word in the sentences below.

a) Power is the **energy / voltage** transferred per second.

b) Power is measured in **watts / amps**.

c) The power of an appliance tells you how **fast / long** it transfers energy.

Q4 Complete the equations for finding the **power** of an appliance.

Power	=	....	×	Potential Difference
P	=	I	×	....

Electric Current and Power

Q5 Complete the labels on the circuit shown below.

a) The .... measures voltage or potential difference.

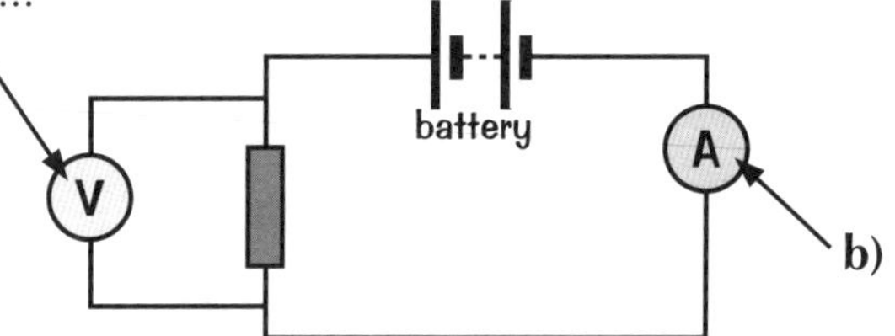

b) The .... measures current.

Example: A TV has a potential difference of **230 V**. It has a current of **3.1 A**. Calculate the **power** of the TV. Give the correct units in your answer.

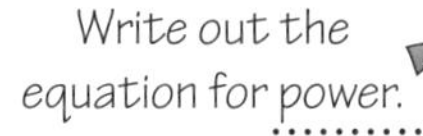

power = current × potential difference

power = 3.1 A × 230 V = 713 W

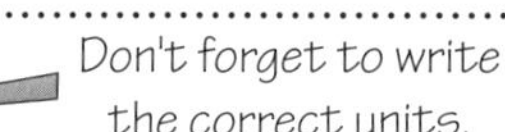

Plug the numbers in.

Work out the answer with a calculator.

Q6 Lamps A and B have a potential difference of **230 V**.

power = current × potential difference

a) **Lamp A** has a current of **4 A.** Calculate the **power** of Lamp A in **watts**.

....

....

b) The power of **Lamp B** is 100 W. Which lamp transfers the **most energy per second**? Circle the answer.

Lamp A **Lamp B**

Q7 The potential difference for the appliances in the table below is **230 V**. Calculate the power of each one. Write the answers in the table.

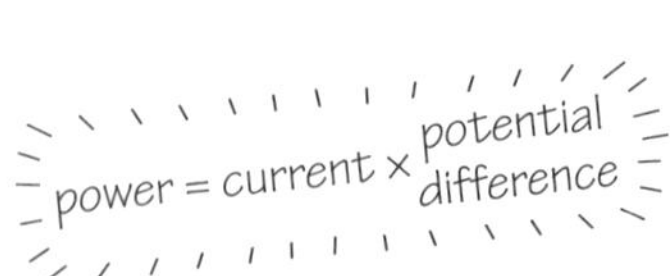

Appliance	Current (A)	Power (W)
Kettle	11.3	2600
Radio	0.05	
Laptop computer	3.2	
Lamp	0.25	

Generating Electricity

Q1 Complete the sentences about generating electricity. Use the words listed below them.

a) Moving a magnet in or near a coil of wire makes a .... flow in the wire.

current magnet ammeter

b) This is called ....

destruction instruction induction

c) Generators make a(n) .... current.

direct straight alternating

d) Dynamos are .... generators.

small-scale large-scale powerful

Q2 You can make a **current** by moving a magnet near a coil of wire.

Circle the **four** things below that would **increase** the size of the current.

Moving the magnet faster

Using a stronger magnet

Having fewer turns on the coil

Increasing the area of the coil

Moving the magnet slower

Using a weaker magnet

Having more turns on the coil

Generating Electricity

Q3 A generator makes electricity using a magnet and a coil of wire. How will changing each of the things below affect the current? Tick the right answer.

	Larger current	Smaller current	Same current
a) More turns on the coil.	☐	☐	☐
b) Stronger magnet.	☐	☐	☐
c) Slower movement.	☐	☐	☐

Q4 Complete the labels on the diagram of a **generator**.
Use words from the box. One has been done for you.

~~turbine~~	coil of wire	current	magnetic field inside generator

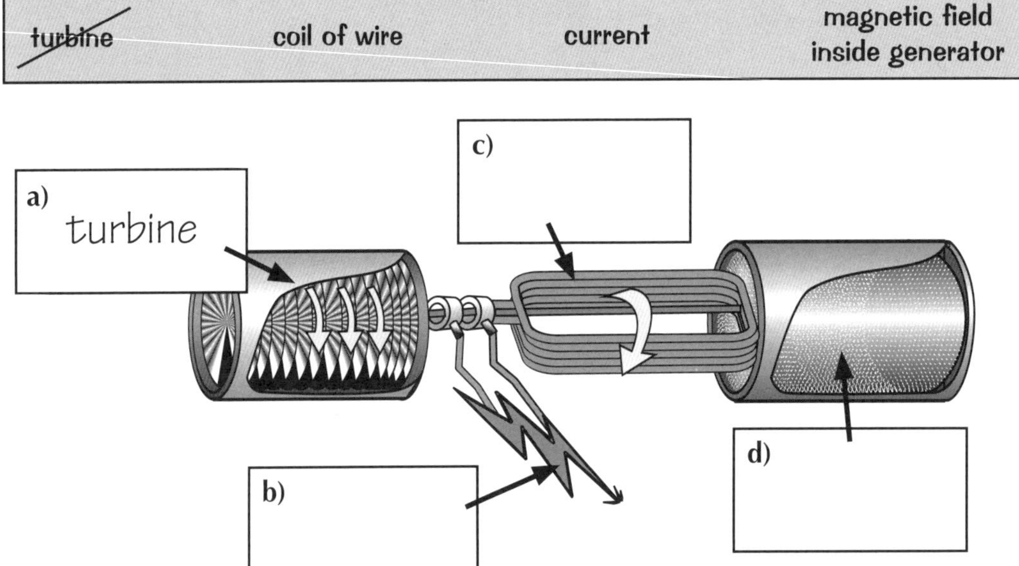

Q5 Circle the right words in the sentences below.

Magnets have a **magnetic** / **electric** field.

The field changes if it is **moved** / **held still** inside a coil of wire.

The change makes a current if the coil is in a **circuit** / **straight line**.

You can change the direction of the current by moving the magnet **faster** / **in the other direction**.

You can also change the **direction** / **size** of the current by putting the magnet through the coil the other end first.

Non-Renewable Energy Resources

Q1 Are these sentences **true** or **false**? Tick the boxes.

		True	False
a)	Coal and gas are both non-renewable energy sources.	☐	☐
b)	Non-renewable energy sources will never run out.	☐	☐
c)	Most power stations use steam to drive a turbine to generate electricity.	☐	☐
d)	Burning fossil fuels doesn't damage the environment.	☐	☐

Q2 Draw lines to match up each problem below with something that causes it.

Acid rain	Giving out carbon dioxide by burning fossil fuels
Climate change	Coal mining
Dangerous nuclear waste	Sulfur dioxide made by burning oil and coal
Making a mess of the landscape	Using nuclear power

Q3 Complete the sentences below using words from the box.

nuclear	burnt	reaction	fossil

a) Coal, oil and gas are .... fuels.

They are .... to make heat.

b) Uranium and plutonium are .... fuels.

They make heat from a nuclear ....

Q4 Non-renewable energy resources have good and bad points. Circle the **good** points.

All the fuels are pretty cheap.

Coal and oil give out sulfur dioxide that causes acid rain.

Nuclear fuels don't give off carbon dioxide — so they don't add to climate change.

Coal mining makes a mess of the landscape.

They produce lots of energy.

Fossil fuels give out carbon dioxide when burnt which adds to climate change.

Nuclear waste is very dangerous and hard to get rid of.

Using Renewable Energy Resources (1)

Q1 Tick **two** boxes to show two **good** points of renewable energy resources.

- [ ] Some are unreliable as they depend on the weather.
- [ ] Most don't need a fuel so they have low running costs.
- [ ] They will never run out.
- [ ] They don't give out as much energy as non-renewables.

Q2 Complete the table to show the good and bad points of renewable energy resources. Use words from the list.

Wave power   Tidal power   Hydroelectricity

RENEWABLE RESOURCE	GOOD POINT	BAD POINT
	Useful on small islands.	Won't work when the wind drops.
	Very reliable.	Can only be used in certain places.
	Electricity can be made whenever it's needed.	Flooding can destroy wildlife habitats.

Q3 Are these sentences describing **hydroelectricity**, **tidal** power or **both**? Tick the boxes.

	Hydroelectricity	Tidal	Both
a) It is usually used across rivers.	☐	☐	☐
b) The power stations are expensive to build.	☐	☐	☐
c) It can provide electricity when you need it.	☐	☐	☐
d) Electricity is made by spinning a turbine.	☐	☐	☐

Q4 Complete the labels on the diagram of a **hydroelectric power station**. Use sentences from the box.

a)

b)

c)

A dam catches and stores rain water.

Water is let out through the turbine.

Valleys are flooded.

Using Renewable Energy Resources (2)

Q1 Circle the right words to complete the sentences on **solar cells**.

Solar cells make electricity from **sunlight** / **moonlight**.

They are very **reliable / unreliable** in sunny places.

They are often used in very **remote / crowded** places like mountains.

They don't work **at night** / **during the day** or when it's cloudy.

Q2 **Wind power** has good and bad points. Tick the **good** points.

- ☐ It can be used on a large scale.
- ☐ Turbines spoil the view.
- ☐ Turbines can be very noisy.
- ☐ There's no pollution.
- ☐ They only work when it's windy.

Q3 Circle the sentences below that are **good points** about **geothermal energy**.

It's cheap to run.

There aren't many places you can do it.

It costs a lot to drill down to the hot rocks.

There are no environmental problems.

Q4 Complete the sentences about **biomass**. Use words from the box below.

growing	carbon dioxide	farm waste	burnt

a) Biomass is .... in power stations.

b) It can be made from landfill rubbish, ... , animal poo and special forests.

c) It doesn't add to the overall amount of .... in the air.

d) Plants and animals can lose their homes to make room for .... biomass.

Comparison of Energy Resources

Q1 Which of the sentences below are **true**? Tick the boxes.

- Renewable energy resources that use the weather are reliable. ☐
- Non-renewable energy resources are reliable. ☐
- Non-renewable energy resources cause pollution. ☐
- Hydroelectric dams, tidal barrages and nuclear power stations are the least expensive to build. ☐

Q2 a) Which type of energy resource usually has the **highest running costs**? Tick the box.

☐ Renewable ☐ Non-renewable

b) Circle the sentence below that explains your answer to **a)**.

The fuel is more expensive.

It doesn't make enough electricity.

People have to be paid more to work there.

Q3 Draw lines to match up the type of power station with its **location**.

geothermal	away from people and near water
hydroelectricity	hilly, rainy places
nuclear	near a coal mine
coal	volcanic places

Q4 Complete the table by adding the energy resources below to the first column.

hydroelectricity nuclear gas

	Energy resource	Bad points
a)		It causes pollution. It will run out eventually. The power stations are noisy and spoil the view.
b)		It will run out eventually. It makes dangerous waste. The power stations are very expensive to build.
c)		It can harm wildlife. The dam could burst and cause damage. It can spoil the view.

Electricity and the National Grid

Q1 This is a diagram of the **National Grid**. Label the diagram with the words in the box.

pylons	step-up transformer	power station	step-down transformer

a) ....

c) ....

b) ....

d) ....

Q2 Circle the right words in the sentences.

Electricity travels through the National Grid at a **high** / **low** voltage.

Electricity travels through the National grid at **high** / **low** current.

This helps to **increase** / **decrease** the energy that is lost as heat.

This means that electricity costs **less** / **more** and it improves efficiency.

Q3 Are the sentences below **true** or **false**? Tick the boxes.

		True	False
a)	Transformers can be used to increase voltage.	☐	☐
b)	Transformers can be used to decrease voltage.	☐	☐
c)	Transformers can only change the size of a direct current.	☐	☐
d)	In the National Grid, transformers increase the voltage to a safe level before we use it.	☐	☐

Q4 Give **one** reason why people might be worried about living near high voltage power lines.

....

....

Energy & Cost-Efficiency (1)

Q1 Circle the right word in the sentences below.

a) Insulating your home means keeping **water** / **heat** inside.

b) Insulation **increases** / **decreases** your energy bills.

c) Insulating your house **is free** / **costs money**.

Q2 The **payback time** for insulation isn't always the same.

a) What is the payback time? Circle the right answer.

When the money spent on insulation is more than twice your energy bill.

When the money saved on bills is £1000.

When the money saved on bills is the same as the money spent on insulation.

b) Complete the sentences using the words above the box.

good shorter bad longer

> The .... the payback time for something, the more cost-efficient it is. This just means it's .... value for money.

Q3 The table below shows information about a hot water tank jacket and loft insulation.

	Hot water tank jacket	Loft insulation
Initial Cost	£60	£200
Annual Saving	£15	£100
Payback time = initial cost ÷ annual saving	60 ÷ 15 = 4 years	.... ÷ .... = ... years

a) Complete the table by calculating the **payback time** for **loft insulation**.

b) Which insulation is better value for money? Circle the answer.

Hot water tank jacket Both equally good value Loft insulation

Energy & Cost-Efficiency (2)

Q1 Which of these sentences about low-energy appliances are **true**? Tick the boxes.

Low-energy appliances use less energy to do the same job as other ones. ☐

They can also be called energy-saving or efficient appliances. ☐

They are more expensive to run than other appliances. ☐

They can be more expensive to buy than other appliances. ☐

Q2 A kettle has a power of **2 kW**.

a) What is its power in **watts**? Tick the box next to the right answer.

☐ 2 W ☐ 200 W ☐ 2000 W

b) The kettle runs off energy from the mains supply. What **units** is this energy measured in?

☐ kilowatt-hours ☐ watts ☐ joules

Q3 The **power** of an appliance is how much electricity it uses over a certain time.

a) A hair dryer uses **120 000 J** of energy in **120 seconds**.
Complete the calculation to find the power of the hair dryer.

Power (W) = Energy (J) ÷ Time (s)

= .... ÷ ....

= .... W

b) Write down the power of the hair dryer in **kW**.

....

Q4 An electricity company charges **7 pence per kilowatt-hour**.
Calculate how much it costs to leave a **0.5 kW** washing machine on for **2 hours**.

Cost of energy = power × time × cost of 1 kilowatt-hour

= .... × .... × 7p

= .... p

Energy Transfer (1)

Q1 Draw lines to match each **type** of energy to its description. One has been done for you.

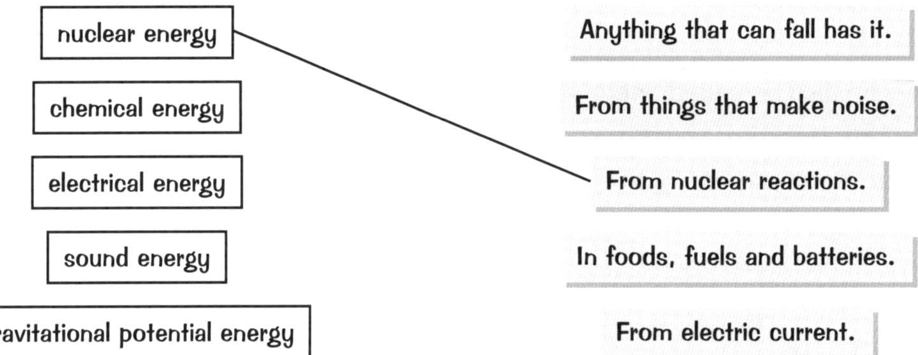

Q2 Complete the sentences. Use words from the list.

change made conserved

Energy is always ....

Energy can never be .... or got rid of.

Energy can only ever .... from one type to another.

Q3 Complete the **energy transfer chains** below. Use words from the box.

light	electrical	sound	elastic potential	chemical

a) Gas cooker: .... energy → heat energy

b) Electric buzzer: electrical energy → .... energy

c) Wind-up toy car: .... energy → kinetic energy

Q4

Bruce is lifting a weight.

a) Bruce holds the weight **still** above his head.
What **type of energy** does the weight have? Circle the answer.

nuclear energy gravitational potential energy light energy

b) Bruce **lets go** and the weight falls.
What type of energy does the weight have as it falls? Circle the answer.

kinetic energy light energy sound energy

Energy Transfer (2)

Q1 Are the sentences **true** or **false**? Tick the boxes.

		True	False
a)	Efficiency is the share of the energy put in that is transferred into useful energy.	☐	☐
b)	The energy a machine transfers that's not useful is called wasted energy.	☐	☐
c)	The more efficient a machine is, the more energy it wastes.	☐	☐
d)	The total energy given out by a machine is always the same as the energy put in.	☐	☐

Q2 Draw lines to match each object with its **useful energy change**. One has been done for you.

Object:	Useful energy change:
car	electrical → heat
light bulb	chemical → kinetic
iron	chemical → electrical
battery	electrical → light

Q3 Here is an **energy transfer diagram** for an electric lamp.

energy in 100 J
light energy out 5 J
heat energy out

Complete the sentences below. Use the diagram to help.

a) The **total energy in** is .... J

b) The amount of **useful energy** is .... J

c) The amount of energy **wasted** is .... J

Q4 a) Complete the **efficiency** formula below. Use words from the list.

total energy efficiency useful energy

$$\text{............} = \frac{\text{............}}{\text{............}} \times 100\%$$

b) Use the **efficiency formula** to complete the table below. One has been done for you.

Total Energy (J)	Useful Energy (J)	Efficiency (%)
200	20	10
4000	2000	
4000	1000	

Heat Energy

Q1 Are these sentences **true** or **false**? Tick the boxes.

		True	False
a)	Hotter objects radiate more heat than they absorb.	☐	☐
b)	Cooler objects absorb less heat than they radiate.	☐	☐
c)	The rate of energy change is called efficiency.	☐	☐
d)	If the power of heat absorbed is the same as the power radiated, the temperature will stay the same.	☐	☐

Q2 Circle the right words in the sentences below.

a) **Dark and matt / Bright and shiny** surfaces are the **best** at absorbing and radiating heat.

b) **Dark and matt / Bright and shiny** surfaces are the **worst** at absorbing and radiating heat.

Q3 Tim filled a **Leslie's cube** with hot water.
He then measured the temperature of each surface.

Draw lines to match each surface to the temperature Tim measured.
One has been done for you.

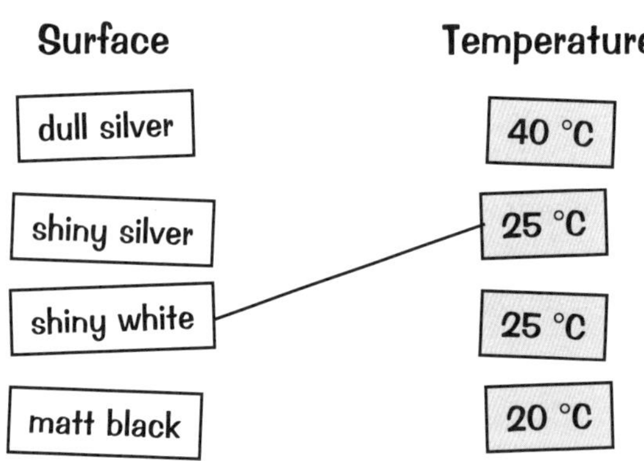

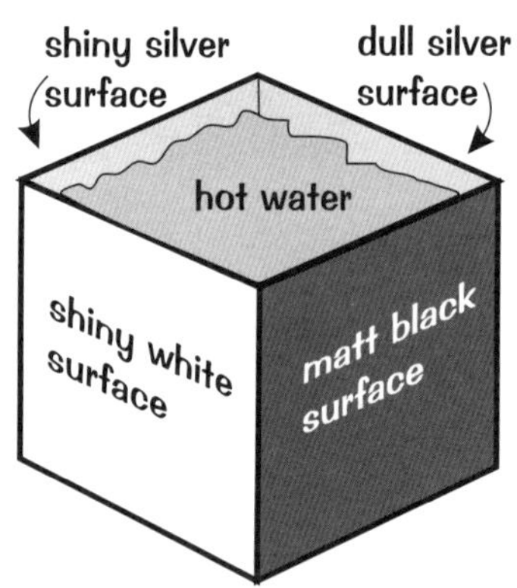

Q4 Ball bearings are stuck onto metal plates with wax, as shown.
The plates are the same distance away from a Bunsen burner.

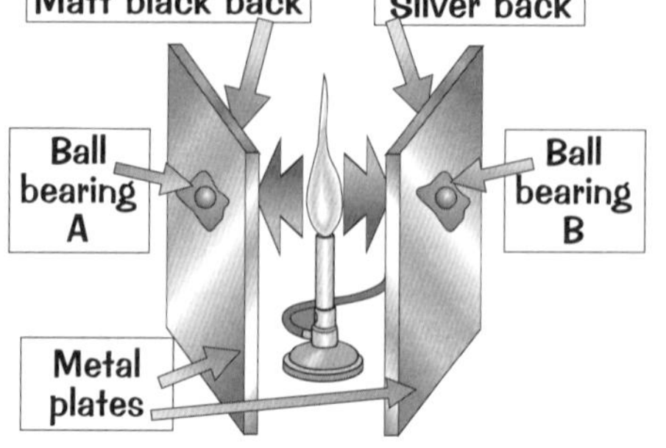

a) Which ball bearing will drop first? Circle the answer.

Ball bearing A **Ball bearing B**

b) **Why** does this ball bearing drop first?

....

....

Mixed Questions — P1b Topics 4, 5 & 6

Q1 Earthquakes cause **P-waves** and **S-waves**.

a) Are P-waves longitudinal or transverse? Circle the answer.

longitudinal transverse

b) Are S-waves longitudinal or transverse? Circle the answer.

longitudinal transverse

c) What causes earthquakes? Circle the answer.

tectonic plates sliding past each other seismic waves hydroelectric power

Q2 A sheep farmer uses **solar cells** to make electricity.

a) Why are solar cells are a good way of making electricity? Circle the answer.

A — They are reliable in sunny places in the daytime. B — They can make electricity whenever it's needed.

b) The farmer uses the electricity to power his TV.
Complete the energy transfer chain for the TV. Use words from the list.

electrical energy kinetic energy light energy chemical energy

.... → .... + sound energy + heat energy

c) The farmer lives on an island.
Name **two other** renewable resources he could use to make electricity.

1. ....

2. ....

Q3 Sound waves can have different frequencies.

a) What are the frequency ranges for ultrasound and infrasound waves? Tick the boxes.

Ultrasound: ☐ below 20 hertz ☐ 20 - 20 000 hertz ☐ higher than 20 000 hertz

Infrasound: ☐ below 20 hertz ☐ 20 - 20 000 hertz ☐ higher than 20 000 hertz

b) Give **one** example of how we can use ultrasound waves.

....

Mixed Questions — P1b Topics 4, 5 & 6

Q4 John has a lamp. The potential difference across the lamp is **6 V**. The current is **5 A**.

a) What is the **power** of the lamp? Circle the answer.

power = current × potential difference

50 W   6 W   2 W   30 W

b) Another lamp has a power of **0.05 kW**. The cost of electricity is **10p per kWh**.
Complete the calculation to find the cost of using this lamp for **24 hours**.

Cost = Power × Time × Cost of 1 kWh

= .... × .... × ....

= ....

Don't forget to give the units.

c) John spends **£10** on a new bulb for his lamp which will save him **£2** a year on his energy bills.
Complete the calculation to find the **payback time** for the new bulb.

Payback Time = Initial Cost ÷ Annual Saving

Payback Time = ... ÷ ....

Payback Time = ... years

d) Bulb X has a payback time of **5 years**. Bulb Y has a payback time of **3 years**.
Which bulb is more cost-efficient, bulb X or bulb Y?

....

Q5 For every **1000 J** of energy put **in** to a power station, **600 J** is **wasted**.

a) Calculate the energy transferred into **useful** energy in this power station.

useful energy = total energy − wasted energy

....

....

b) Calculate the **efficiency** of this power station.

$\text{efficiency} = \frac{\text{useful energy}}{\text{total energy}} \times 100\%$

....

....

c) Electricity is carried from power stations by cables.
Why is the electricity in these cables at a **high voltage**? Circle the answer.

It makes the current low so you don't lose much energy as heat in the cables.

It makes the current high so you don't lose much energy as heat in the cables.

SFRW41